Indonesians
Portraits from an Archipelago

Indonesians
Portraits from an Archipelago

Photographs by

IAN CHARLES STEWART

Text by

IAN CHARLES STEWART & JUDITH SHAW

INDONESIA
PARAMOUNT CIPTA
CONCEPT MEDIA
SINGAPORE

Photo editors: Ian Charles Stewart & Hasan-Uddin Khan
Art director: Hasan-Uddin Khan
Designers: Design Objectives Pte Ltd

Production coordinator: Patricia Theseira
Typesetting by Computype Pte Ltd
Colour separations by Colourscan Co Pte Ltd
Printed and bound in Singapore by Tien Wah Press (Pte) Ltd

Photographs by Ian Charles Stewart
except those on pages 184 & 185 by Gene Christy
and on page 184 by Nora Suryanti
and on pages 216, 217 & 218 by Virginia White
and on page 218 by Edith Somerset
Text by Ian Charles Stewart and Judith Shaw
Preface by H. Mahendra

Published by Concept Media Pte Ltd,
19 Tanglin Road, #06-52, Singapore 1024 and
Paramount Cipta Ltd, P.O. Box 280,
KBY Jakarta Selatan, Indonesia.
First printing — October 1983
Second printing — April 1984
Photographs: © Yayasan Bhakti Putra.
Book: © Paramount Cipta & Concept Media.

ISBN: 9971-83-772-2

CONTENTS

Preface

Indonesia has long been looked upon as a country of great scenic beauty and a wealth of natural resources. Both are true, but greater resources and a much warmer beauty can be found in the people of this vast land. The motivating force behind the decision to create *Indonesians: Portraits from an Archipelago* is the wish to share, particularly with non-Indonesian readers, this as yet unrecognised but abundantly visible wealth.

This book is about people, the many different peoples who live on the islands of the Indonesian archipelago. It offers a composite portrait of the many different environments and cultural backgrounds that co-exist here, as well as the underlying traditions that bind these differing cultures together. These common traditions are based on simplicity, belief in the Good, tolerance, and respect for others. Most important is an all-pervading spiritual sensitivity, and a strong belief in God. Many different religions exist side by side in Indonesia, and most people participate in at least one.

This book is not about the high culture of Indonesia, or the great ceremonies of the royal courts. It portrays ordinary people living their daily lives, much of which is engraved on their faces. The slant is rural rather than urban; low-key rather than dramatic and unusual. It aims at giving the reader an understanding of the country and people as they are today, with their long traditions in tenuous balance with the demands and intrusions of the modern world. Although their ethnological characteristics will not change in the foreseeable future, attitudes, behaviour and way of life are likely to be greatly influenced by the tide of Western-style modernisation sweeping the country. No-one can predict what effect this modernisation will have on peoples with a traditional culture strongly rooted in rural, agricultural society, but certain changes in living patterns are already visible. Thirty years from now this book may portray only the Indonesia of the "good old days".

The concepts and traditions that form the basis of Indonesian culture are different from those underlying Western societies. These differences influence the day-to-day behaviour of the people and are reflected in the photographs in this book.

One of the dominant concepts at all levels of Indonesian society is *gotong royong,* or mutual help, which stresses social unity and the inter-connectedness of people. The Indonesian does not look at himself as an individual in the sense that the term is used in the West. Rather he is part of a group—family, clan, village—and develops his identity in relation to that group. Such deeply entrenched traditions as *gotong royong,* however, today face the challenge of change. Many Indonesians in the big cities have begun to appreciate privacy; some have adopted an individual life style. But the acceptance of *gotong royong* as a principle in national life puts heavy restrictions on the development of too extreme an individualistic outlook among the population in general.

Another strong tradition in Indonesian society is the decision-making process known as *musyawarah untuk mufakat*, "deliberation leading to consensus". In Indonesia, the majority seldom rules; neither are decisions simply handed down from above. Rather the people who must implement the decision reach agreement on the correct path before a decision is taken. This technique is slow but effective, because everyone involved is behind the action decided upon. *Musyawarah untuk mufakat* is the method applied in the People's Consultative Assembly, the House of People's Representatives, the Cabinet, and the Supreme Advisory Council. Voting is only used in Indonesian democracy when no consensus can be reached.

One of the themes of this book is the development, in even the remotest parts of the archipelago, of an emerging Indonesian culture that transcends the differences of the various regions. The national motto is *Bhinneka Tunggal Ika*, "Unity in Diversity". Despite vast cultural diversity, the national identity is becoming stronger all the time. The thrust toward Indonesian cultural unity is not new. In 1331 Gajah Mada, one of the most famous ministers of the Majapahit Kingdom made what has come to be known as the *"Palapa Vow"*, swearing never to rest until the whole archipelago was united under Majapahit rule. Indonesia's telecommunications satellites, which interconnect the entire nation in all its far-flung diversity and also bring Indonesia closer to the rest of world, are named *Palapa* to commemorate his resolve. It is hoped that, in some small measure, this book can do the same.

- H. Mahendra -

8

Introduction

Indonesia is the world's largest archipelago, with more than 13,000 islands stretching over 4,800 kilometres across the seas between Asia and Australia. The six major islands are Sumatra, Java, Bali, Kalimantan, Sulawesi and Irian Jaya. Maluku and Nusa Tenggara, which make up Indonesia's two remaining divisions, are groups of islands running from Sulawesi to Irian in the North and from Bali to Timor in the south. The country is divided into twenty-seven provinces. The two newest are Irian Jaya and East Timor, which joined the Republic in 1969 and 1976 respectively. More than sixty percent of Indonesia's 160 million people live on Java. With the exception of the tiny island of Bali, also densely inhabited, population is relatively sparse throughout the rest of the country, much of which is forest and jungle. Less than half the land is arable.

Indonesia straddles the equator, and the climate is mostly tropical. Rainfall varies, from the semi-arid islands of Nusa Tenggara to the lush rain forests of Sumatra, Kalimantan and Irian Jaya. Irrigated rice fields, called *sawah,* have been used in Java and Bali for thousands of years, and whole societies have grown up around the apportionment and control of water. Wet-rice cultivation occurs on some of the outer islands, where water and suitable land are available. On other islands corn, sago, and cassava are dietary staples. In most areas fish is an important source of protein.

Indonesia is the home of a large variety of plant and animal life, much of it found nowhere else in the world. Among the more unusual species are the orangutans of Kalimantan and North Sumatra, West Java's one-horned rhinoceros, and the dwarf buffalo of Sulawesi. The world's largest flower, the *Rafflesia Arnoldi,* is found here, as are thousands of species of orchid. The "Wallace Line" falls between Bali and the island of Lombok in West Nusa Tenggara. Animals and plants on islands to the west of that line are most clearly related to the flora and fauna of Asia; plant and animal life on islands to the east are similar to those of New Guinea and Australia.

There is a greater wealth of ethnic diversity in Indonesia than perhaps anywhere in the world. More than 300 ethnic groups and about 365 languages co-exist here, although *Bahasa Indonesia,* the national language, is now spoken everywhere. The reason for this incredible variety of peoples lies in Indonesia's position *vis à vis* Asia and Australia. Until relatively recently, geologically speaking, Indonesia was connected to Asia and Australia by three land bridges. Sumatra, Java, Bali and Kalimantan were one land mass extending north into peninsular Malaysia and Indo-China; Sulawesi was connected to the Philippines and north to Taiwan and Japan; New Guinea and Australia were also joined. Primitive humans, along with many species of animal, were able to walk into what is now Indonesia from Asia. Fossil remains of Java Man, an upright-striding hominid, date back at least one million years. Time brought more sophisticated cultures to Indonesia, as well as stone-age technology. When the ice age ended in Europe, Indonesia was no longer connected to the mainland. Waves of migrants came by boat from China, Thailand and Vietnam. Reflections of these cultures can be seen in bronze drums and gongs, polished ceremonial tools, and designs still vibrant in Indonesian decorative arts today.

Although enjoying sporadic periods of unifying cultural influence—under the Sriwijaya Kingdom in the 12th and 13th Centuries, and the 14th-Century Majapahit Kingdom, for instance—the different areas of the archipelago were often politically fragmented. Islam, which entered the islands in the 13th Century, was a strong unifying factor; today the vast majority of Indonesians are Muslim. The era of European influence began in the 16th Century when the Portuguese arrived in Maluku. They were followed by the Dutch in the 17th Century and the English, who ruled Indonesia for a few years from 1811-1816. The Dutch were the major colonial power in the archipelago, exercising control first through the Dutch East India Company, established in 1602 and later through the Dutch government.

In 1945 Sukarno and Mohammad Hatta proclaimed Indonesia's independence. After nearly five years of guerilla war against the Dutch, Indonesia was recognised as an independent, sovereign nation in the final days of 1949. Sukarno was Indonesia's first President from 1950 to 1965. The "New Order", under President Suharto, began in 1968. He was elected for a third term in 1983.

Indonesia's national philosophy, *Pancasila*, is embodied in the preamble to the 1945 Constitution. Its five points are "Belief in the One Supreme God; Just and Civilised Humanity; Unity of Indonesia; The People's Sovereignty guided by the wisdom of unanimity in deliberation among representatives; and Social Justice for all the people of Indonesia".

Young men in ceremonial dress, Nusa Tenggara.

10

Andaman Sea

South China Sea

BRUNEI

• Banda
Aceh

MALAYSIA

Medan •

Strait of Malacca

MALAYSIA

Mt Menyapa
▲ 2000

SIMEULUE

Lake Toba

SINGAPORE

R. Mahakam

NIAS

Pekanbaru •

Pontianak •

KALIMANTAN

SUMATRA

R. Kapuas

Balikpapan •

• Padang

MENTAWAI ISLANDS

R. Barito

Makassar Stra

▲ Gunung Kerinci
3800

BANGKA

Palembang •

Banjarmasin

Indian Ocean

Java Sea

Sunda Strait

• Jakarta

MADURA

• Bandung

• Surakarta • Surabaya

• Yogyakarta

▲ Mt Bromo
2392

BALI

JAVA

LOMBOK

SUMBAW

Indian Ocean

Indonesia

The maps at the beginning of every
chapter indicate the places shown
in the photographs. Major islands,
cities and towns are also given, but
much has been omitted in the
interest of clarity.

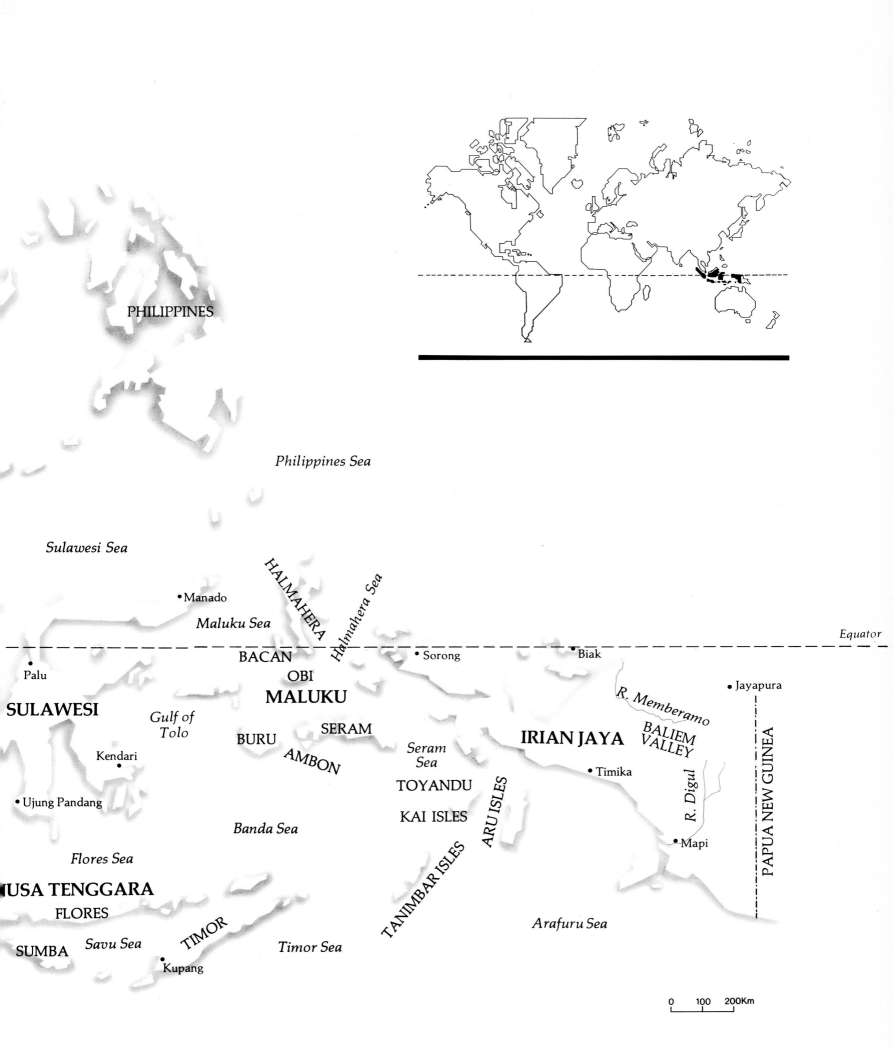

PHILIPPINES

Philippines Sea

Sulawesi Sea

• Manado

HALMAHERA

Halmahera Sea

Maluku Sea

Equator

BACAN

• Sorong

• Biak

• Palu

OBI

MALUKU

• Jayapura

SULAWESI

Gulf of Tolo

BURU

SERAM

R. Memberamo

IRIAN JAYA

BALIEM VALLEY

AMBON

Seram Sea

Kendari •

• Timika

PAPUA NEW GUINEA

• Ujung Pandang

TOYANDU

KAI ISLES

ARU ISLES

R. Digul

Banda Sea

• Mapi

Flores Sea

TANIMBAR ISLES

NUSA TENGGARA

FLORES

Arafuru Sea

SUMBA

Savu Sea

TIMOR

Timor Sea

• Kupang

0   100   200Km

Sumatra

Sumatra. An island where tigers, elephants and rhinos still roam the forests; where head-hunters have only just left off their bloodthirsty purusits. Sumatra's northern tip faces India, its northeast coast borders Malaysia and the Strait of Malacca, and across the Sunda Strait Java is less than twenty-five kilometres away. The fifth largest island in the world, Sumatra is a land of coastal swamps, inland mountain chains, crater lakes, and thousands of square kilometres of nearly impenetrable jungle. Natural resources are plentiful: Sumatra exports oil, natural gas and tropical hardwoods, as well as the rubber, coffee, sugar, palm oil and tobacco that have been grown here for centuries.

Ideally located as a port of call for Asian travellers, Sumatra has a long history of foreign contact. The first visitors walked in more than a million years ago when Sumatra, Java and Bali were connected to the mainland. Groups of primitive humans, *Homo Erectus* and early *Homo Sapiens* drifted south from China and Southeast Asia. Some of these migrants settled in Sumatra; others moved on to Java or across to western Borneo. Millennia passed. Neolithic peoples from China and what is now Vietnam came by boat, bringing agriculture, pottery, and metal-working technology with them. They settled in Sumatra, mixing with the local people or driving them inland. More migrants came and the cycle was repeated again and again, continuing well into the modern era.

Today, Sumatra is the home of many different peoples. The tall, dark-skinned dignified Acehnese in the north; the Batak people of Lake Toba, the creative, shrewd Minangkabau and the Kubu of the south, whose lives are scarcely different from their nomadic stone-age forebears. Together with the island's other ethnic groups they present a richly varied tapestry of race and culture.

Aceh, Sumatra's northernmost province, first appeared in historical records as the 6th-Century Buddhist State of Poli. By the time Marco Polo reached the area, it was already strongly Muslim. A people whose lifeblood is trade, it is no surprise that they enthusiastically embraced this religion, brought by traders. But Islam in Aceh, though always visible, is understated and has been, to a certain extent, adapted to fit local needs. This flexibility of religious interpretation is characteristic of Indonesia as a whole and can be seen throughout the archipelago in varying degrees.

Nias is an island about 120 kilometres off the west coast of North Sumatra. The Niah were valued as slaves on Sumatra, especially by the Acehnese, and slave raids were common on the island. In addition, the Niah were enthusiastic fighters and head-hunters, and villages were often at war with one another. Niasan architecture reflects a very real need for defense. Houses are strongly fortified, with barred windows and trap-door entrances through the

A devout young girl in Muslim dress praying.

15

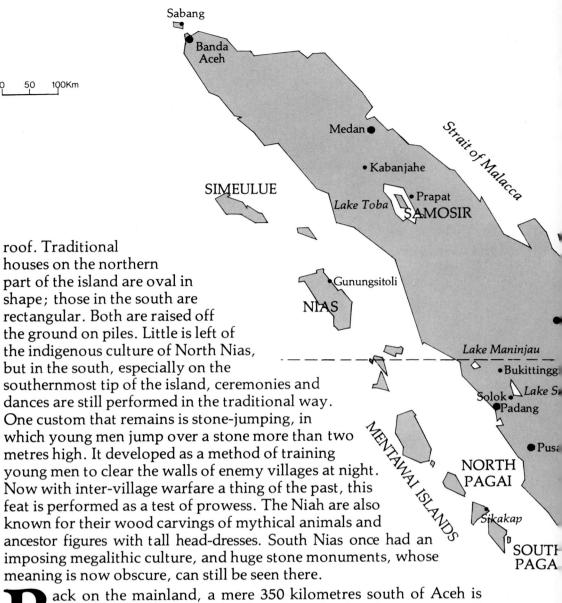

roof. Traditional
houses on the northern
part of the island are oval in
shape; those in the south are
rectangular. Both are raised off
the ground on piles. Little is left of
the indigenous culture of North Nias,
but in the south, especially on the
southernmost tip of the island, ceremonies and
dances are still performed in the traditional way.
One custom that remains is stone-jumping, in
which young men jump over a stone more than two
metres high. It developed as a method of training
young men to clear the walls of enemy villages at night.
Now with inter-village warfare a thing of the past, this
feat is performed as a test of prowess. The Niah are also
known for their wood carvings of mythical animals and
ancestor figures with tall head-dresses. South Nias once had an
imposing megalithic culture, and huge stone monuments, whose
meaning is now obscure, can still be seen there.

Back on the mainland, a mere 350 kilometres south of Aceh is
the land of the Tapanuli, whose heartland is the area around
Lake Toba in North Sumatra. Called Batak by outsiders, they
have maintained their cultural identity although surrounded on all
sides by people with very different traditions. There are six Batak
subgroups, with the Toba, Karo and Mandailing being the largest. All
Batak groups share a basic language and similar culture, although
minor differences are evident. They have in common, however, a
reputation for plain speaking that is notorious throughout Indonesia.
Unlike the refined Javanese who hides his feelings behind a mask of
good manners, the Batak always says what he means.

South of Batakland in the area around Bukittinggi live the
people known as Minangkabau. Intensely Muslim, the Minangkabau
have a social system in which name and control of property pass
down through the female line. It used to be the case that when a
woman married, the groom either moved in with her family or, if he
preferred, only visited at first, gradually moving in his belongings as
the relationship became established. If there were marital difficulties,
he would gradually move them out again. Today marriage customs
among the Minangkabau are not very different from marriage
customs elsewhere in Sumatra, although they are still usually
matrilocal. Management of the family fields is the responsibility of the
women; a Minangkabau man is more likely to be found working the
land of his mother or sister than that of his wife's family. It may seem
strange that a patriarchal religion like Islam should exist comfortably

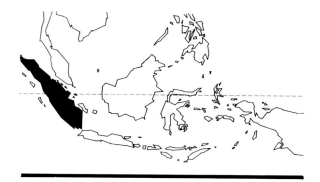

in such a strongly woman-oriented society, but in fact much of pre-Islamic Sumatra shows evidence of the same social organisation. In Aceh marriages are often matrilocal, with the bride staying in her own village after marriage rather than moving to the home of her husband's family. In the area around Mt. Kerinci in South Sumatra the system is strictly matrilineal and matrilocal. A father there is not influential in the affairs of his children, but rather is an important figure to his sister's children.

The Minangkabau people are excellent craftsmen and business people. They are also active in national politics and a high proportion of government officials and civil servants come from this part of Sumatra.

The Mentawai islands lie south of Nias and include the islands of North and South Pagai. More primitive than their neighbours to the north, the Pagai islanders have a history in which weaving, metal-working and domesticated animals played no part. This lack of development can be explained in terms of *punen*, holy periods, which could last anywhere from a few days or weeks to several years. During *punen* most purposeful activity was taboo, including all work in the fields. Food had to be gathered wild or stolen from other villages. Obviously, agricultural pursuits requiring sustained effort, such as growing rice or caring for animals, were not possible. Taro was the staple food, supplemented with yams, banana, sugarcane, durian and fish. Today, *punen* has virtually disappeared, and is observed only on Sundays. During the past few decades, rice cultivation has been developed with the encouragement of missionaries and government officials. Contact with the outside world has increased with the development of a timber industry, and the ancient ways are quickly being lost. The grass skirts so prevalent even ten years ago have now given way to batik sarongs and Western clothing.

In the eastern coastal region live the Kubu, the most primitive of Sumatra's many ethnic groups. Similar in lifestyle to some of the island's earliest inhabitants, they wander in small family groups through the forests between Jambi and Palembang, trading simple woven products for food. Their houses, used for only a few weeks or months and then abandoned, are made of bamboo and palm fronds raised from the ground on bamboo piles. As logging and oil exploration have become more intense in the region, the government has addressed itself to the problems of a country rapidly modernising around these people. Small resettlement villages have been set up at the forests' edge in the hope that some Kubu will give up their nomadic ways and learn to live a more settled way of life.

Sumatra serves as a fitting introduction to Indonesia as a whole because it exhibits many of the contrasting—and sometimes conflicting—features that characterise this rapidly changing nation. Modern bustling cities cheek by jowl with deep jungle, a rich variety of ethnic groups, advanced technology and primitive life-styles, and a wide range of religious beliefs. Sumatra, with one foot firmly planted in traditional culture, is moving quickly into the modern age.

A Minangkabau wedding procession displays a charming mixture of old and new. The bride wears traditional West Sumatran wedding garb with its distinctive golden head-dress, while her attendants cover their heads in the Muslim style.

Minangkabau society, although intensely Muslim, is both matrilineal and matrilocal: descent, name, and property are passed down from mother to daughter. When a woman marries, the groom is invited to live·with the bride's parents, and, if the family can afford it, a new room is added on to house the young couple.

OVERLEAF: *A village landscape near Bukittinggi, West Sumatra. The Minangkabau house in the left foreground shows new extensions.*

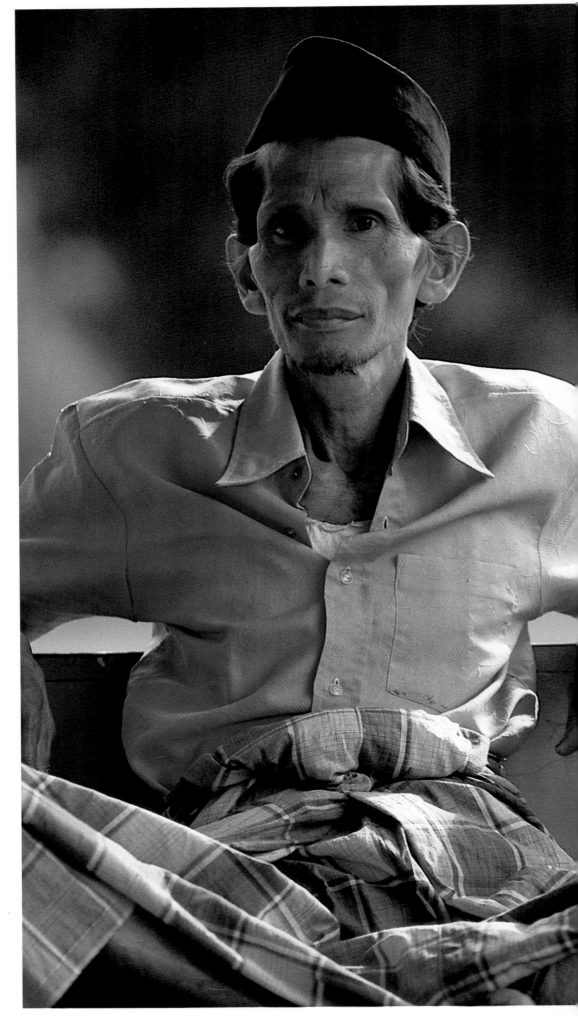

Two men from Aceh sitting in their cool open mosque. Islam was brought to Indonesia in the 13th Century by traders from the Middle East. The first converts were made in Aceh, North Sumatra, and the Acehnese are still considered some of the strictest adherants of Islam in the country.

In Indonesia, unlike many Muslim countries, women are permitted to pray inside the mosque, although they sit apart from the men. These young women wear the obligatory white kerundung which covers everything except the worshiper's face—even hands and feet must be covered. The main mosque at Banda Aceh shows a wealth of intricate detail and a mixture of styles from Arabia, India and Malaysia. As in all mosques, no human or animal forms are portrayed.

Aceh was once famous for its fine unglazed pottery. The craft is still practised, but to a much lesser degree. Here a potter puts the finishing touches on a group of earthenware bowls. They will dry in the sun before being fired in a home-made kiln. The finished bowls are packed in baskets and taken to market by local transport—in this case, by bicycle.

Living on a small island about 120 kilometres off the west coast of North Sumatra, the people of Nias, like this man (top right), can dream idly of the outside world without having it thrust upon them. They have been able to make a more relaxed adjustment to change than their neighbours on the mainland. A Niah girl (above) takes a break from tending her garden; and a family relaxes in the shade of the entrance porch of their house. This young woman (right) wears a modern version of traditional Niasan ceremonial dress.

Mother and child peer out at the world through barred windows. Although not found on modern houses, these horizontal slats are seen on the windows of all older buildings on North and South Nias. This house (above) shows the high sloping roof and skylight windows typical of indigenous Niasan architecture. A modern extension has been added to the right. Seen from the inside, the house is spartan but hospitable. It has three small bedrooms, a kitchen and a large family room. Today more and more people are foregoing the raised houses of their ancestors in favour of conventional houses on the ground.

The village's only store supplies the needs of the entire area. Intricate designs on woven flaxen walls, buffalo horns and two-tiered roof identify this house as belonging to Karo Batak, a group living between Medan and Lake Toba. Like houses found on Nias, Karo houses are raised off the ground on stilts. The verandahs of these houses are versatile. On this one (top) a mother gives her baby a bath.

A Karo woman, her mouth red from chewing betel nut, wears the traditional Batak ulos or shoulder cloth.

Guests arrive for a Karo wedding
bearing gifts. Kampung Lingga's
normal population of about two
hundred swelled to six times that
number as friends and relatives
came from all over the province.
The bride and groom and their
close family members are in the
centre. A closer look at the bride
(above), who is wearing the Batak
head-dress called uis nipes.

Lighting a cigarette, a Karo man watches the wedding go by from a quiet corner. The coffee house where he sits serves as a meeting place for the men of the village. They sip coffee, smoke kretek, Indonesia's clove-scented cigarettes, and chat. Sometimes silent, more often ringing with heated debate, the coffee house is the Batak equivalent of Britain's neighbourhood pub. Another guest at the wedding (right).

Lake Toba is the ancestral home of the Batak peoples. Nine hundred metres above sea level, it is also Asia's largest crater lake. Prapat (above), on the shores of Lake Toba; (left) another view of the lake.

Toba Batak villages consist of a small number of closely-spaced, multi-family houses bordering one street or yard. The village itself is surrounded by an earthen wall with access at either end. This village on Samosir Island, Lake Toba, has six traditional houses and one of modern design. Like those all over Indonesia, the local barber-shop is simple: a shady tree, a chair, and a reasonably sharp razor.

The Toba Batak did not convert to Islam. Instead the majority are Christian with some animistic practices mixed in. The interior of the Protestant church (far right) on Samosir Island.

A vegetable seller at a market near Padang, West Sumatra. Markets start at dawn while it is still cool and are usually over by 9 or 10 o'clock in the morning.

Wearing a pretty dress and an even prettier smile, this Minangkabau girl stands in front of her family's new house. She is wearing kain songket, a silk textile with a supplementary weft of metallic thread. At one time these cloths were woven with real gold and silver, but now synthetic yarns are widely used. As old cloths deteriorate, however, the precious thread is picked out and used again. Weaving songket is a thriving cottage industry in Sumatra; the same girl (right) weaves her own complicated designs.

39

Rice shoots and the view south from Tabek Patoh. The landscape is dominated by hills and valleys with two main lakes—Maninjau and Singkarak.

Minangkabau houses have horn-shaped sway-backed roofs and walls covered with carved and painted panels. This one at Solok has been lived in for several generations and will be used as long as it is comfortable. Well-tended gardens are also a feature of the houses of the Minangkabau.

A Pagai girl in a faded cotton dress. Until recently the people of this village wore only grass skirts. Contact with outsiders over the last ten years has led to styles that, although more modern, are perhaps less comfortable and certainly more expensive.

A view of the village of Sikakap on North Pagai. This part of the village is new, having sprung up to meet the needs of the nearby timber company. Company workers often marry Pagai women and settle in the village. A ship arrives (below) with supplies. The mountain in the background is Gunung Kerinci.

There are no roads to speak of on the islands of North and South Pagai; the river is the principal means of transport. A Pagai woman (above) paddles to market or perhaps to her household garden. Taro is the staple food, though dry-rice cultivation has been introduced by government groups and missionaries. The mortar and pestle (right) is used for husking rice. Sago, generally used as fodder for pigs and chickens, is used for food in remote areas of South Pagai. Other foods are yams, bananas, sugarcane, durian and some fish. Betel nut is not chewed on Pagai, but the people smoke their own homemade cigars.

A Kubu man from near Jambi. Essentially nomadic hunter-gatherers, the Kubu are found in the area between Jambi and Palembang on Sumatra's east coast.

Because their forests are being destroyed by timber cutting, the government is trying to ease the Kubu into a more settled way of life. A Kubu mother (above) carries her child. The sling, a long rectangular cloth called selendang, is used throughout Indonesia for a multiplicity of carrying purposes. This peaceful looking Kubu woman, with the face of a school headmistress, has only recently moved out of the forest into a resettlement village, as has the young boy (right). His future will be very different from the life his parents lived.

44

Java

Java. The name conjures images of temple ruins, smoking volcanoes and spectacular terraced rice fields, every imaginable shade of green. Winding down the steepest hillsides and covering every square metre that has the water to support it, rice is the back-bone of Java. Because of its intense fertility, Java is the most crowded of the Indonesian islands, and the most intensely cultivated. More than sixty percent of the entire population of Indonesia lives here. It also has the lion's share of industry and technology.

Long before there was a written history to tell of it, wet-rice cultivation was known here, perhaps brought by migrants from the Dongson culture of mainland Asia. Wet rice requires water to flood the fields, water directed by intricate irrigation systems from the rivers to the dry lands between. A highly-structured and authoritarian society evolved on Java to direct and control the flow of water.

When Indian traders came to Java in the 6th Century, the Javanese kings adopted Hinduism, with its divinely sanctioned rule and caste system. Brahman priests were invited to Java. They taught their religion and ritual in the Javanese courts, beginning a period of Indian influence that lasted until Islam gained a firm foothold in the 15th Century. The most important of the Javanese kingdoms was the Majapahit, whose influence and prestige stretched from mainland Southeast Asia all the way to Irian Jaya. The *kraton*, or royal courts of Central Java, are still Majapahit in spirit, and the old religions lie just under the skin of the Muslim Javanese.

Ethnically the island can be divided several ways, but perhaps most conveniently into four major groups: the Javanese of Central and East Java; the Sundanese of West Java; the Tenggerese from the area in East Java around Mount Bromo; and the Madurese. Of these the Javanese are numerically the largest group and, in terms of cultural influence, the most important, although regional differences can allow for further subgrouping among them.

With their cultural heartland in the *kraton* of Surakarta and Yogyakarta, the Javanese of the principalities are known for exquisite *batik*; for the workmanship and supernatural powers of their sacred blades, or *kris*; and for the extreme sophistication of their dance. The Javanese language is elaborate and reflects a complex social system. There are three basic levels of speech in Javanese: *Kromo* is used when speaking to superiors or elders, *Ngoko* is for inferiors or when speaking to equals. The third, *Kromo inggil*, is used in the palaces. The interplay of these levels allows for endless subtlety of speech, especially in defining the relative status of the speakers.

The Javanese are an extremely polite and refined people. Loud displays of emotion and flamboyant behaviour of any kind are considered bad manners. This reserve, coupled with a real unwillingness to make anyone else feel uncomfortable or ashamed, often makes

A young boy from a village on the Dieng Plateau, Central Java.

47

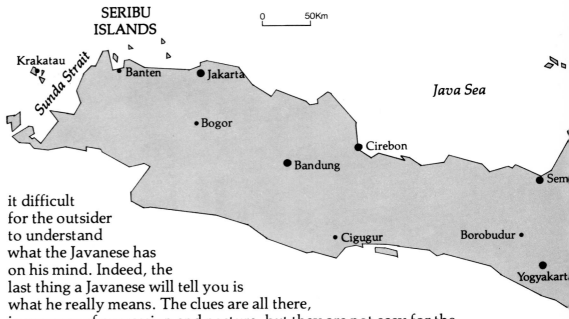

it difficult
for the outsider
to understand
what the Javanese has
on his mind. Indeed, the
last thing a Javanese will tell you is
what he really means. The clues are all there,
in nuances of expression and posture, but they are not easy for the
uninitiated to decipher.

The people of West Java, the Sundanese, are a little less opaque to the outsider's eye, a little less ascetic and perhaps livelier, simpler and less formally structured. If you ask a Sundanese if he is different from a Javanese, the answer is an emphatic affirmative. If you ask how he is different, well, it is difficult to say.

The Badui, a small but distinct ethnic group living in the highlands of West Java, are thought to be a remnant of the original Sundanese people who fled to the mountains and jungles to escape the rising tide of Islam in Java. They have lived in self-imposed isolation since the 15th Century.

Most Javanese and Sundanese follow Islam, but under the surface many old beliefs and traditions persist. The *dukun*, or specialist in magic ritual, is a valued member of the community. There are many kinds of *dukun*. Some specialise in fertility rituals, some are healers of various sorts, some deal with the ghosts and spirits that abound in Java. Still others perform rituals to avert natural disasters. The production and sale of *jamu*, traditional herbal medicine, also is a flourishing business.

The soul of Java is *wayang*, traditional theatre performed with puppets or with actors, using stories from the Hindu epics *Ramayana* or *Mahabharata* to convey a peculiarly Javanese set of values to its audience. To understand Java one must understand *wayang*, but the art form is so subtle, oblique and to the outsider incomprehensible, that one must almost be a Javanese to understand it. There are four basic forms: *wayang kulit* is a shadow play performed with flat leather puppets behind a lamplit screen. *Wayang golek* uses three-dimensional wooden puppets; *wayang topeng* is performed by masked actors; and *wayang orang* or *wong*, the youngest of the forms, is performed by unmasked actors. The oldest and by far the most popular are the shadow puppets.

A set of shadow puppets can contain as many as two hundred pieces, divided into the mostly good characters of the right and the mostly bad characters of the left. There are no absolutes in *wayang*, and although "good" usually triumphs, the victory, more often than not, is ambivalent: a king, for example, who wins a righteous war

48

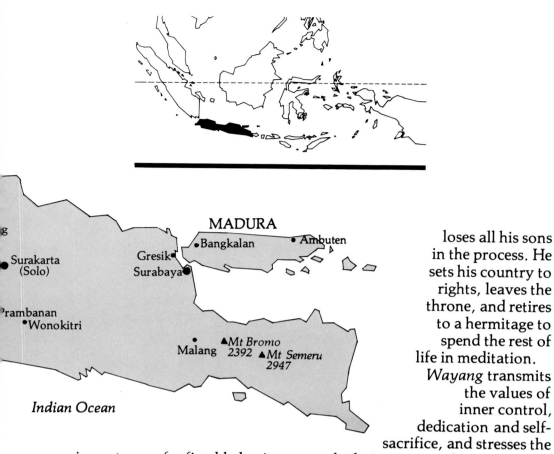

MADURA

Surakarta
(Solo)

Gresik
Surabaya

Bangkalan

Ambuten

Prambanan
Wonokitri

Malang

Mt Bromo
2392
Mt Semeru
2947

Indian Ocean

loses all his sons in the process. He sets his country to rights, leaves the throne, and retires to a hermitage to spend the rest of life in meditation.

Wayang transmits the values of inner control, dedication and self-sacrifice, and stresses the importance of refined behaviour over the boisterous, violent and crude. The Javanese use shadows to illustrate the invisible world and to place themselves in relation to it. The screen is the world, and the puppets exemplify the different roles that can be played in it. The banana trunk, into which the puppets are thrust when not in use, is the surface of the earth; the lamp that lights the screen and projects the flying shadows is the light of life, and the *dalang* or puppeteer is the spirit of God, breathing life into the puppets. *Wayang* has often been called the "Bible of Java", and it is a powerful tool for indoctrination because it is so pervasive and popular. Usually narrated in Javanese or Sundanese, the dialogue is full of slapstick humour as well as pathos, tragedy and serious philosophy. Children grow up with *wayang*. Everyone attends the all-night puppet shows, and children absorb Javanese values as naturally as they breathe. *Wayang* is often used to transmit information to a broad base of people. It has been used in recent years to urge support of a particular political party, for instance, or to encourage the use of modern fertilisers or family planning programmes.

The Tenggerese, an ethnic group which, like the Badui, has isolated itself from the mainstream of Javanese culture, are found in the area between Mount Bromo and Mount Semeru. Mount Bromo was established as a centre for the worship of Brahma during Majapahit times and was largely ignored in the onslaught of Islam. The Tenggerese, however, unlike the Badui, welcome visitors from outside, and their mountains are a popular destination for both Indonesian and foreign tourists.

According to Tengger mythology, a married couple lived on the edge of a huge plain leading down to the sea. They were childless and prayed to the god of the sea for offspring, promising to sacrifice one of their children to the god should their prayers be answered. Years passed and the couple had twenty-five children, but, as is so often the case, they forgot to fulfil their part of the bargain. A pestilence struck the village and many people died. Then the man had a vision, reminding him of his debt, and he summoned all his children to ask which should be sacrificed. Only the youngest child, whose name was Kusuma, offered himself. His father took him down to the edge of the sand and left him there for the god to claim. Immediately, a volcano erupted and Mount Bromo was born. Every year on the fourteenth day of the tenth month, the Tenggerese climb Mount Bromo and throw offerings into the crater to appease the spirit of the volcano and to honour the memory of the child Kusuma.

On Madura, a beautiful but arid island off the northeast coast of Java, live a people having little in common with the East Javanese. Even though many of them have moved to Java itself, they speak a different language, and, because their island does not support much agriculture, live a very different style of life. The raising of cattle, not an important activity on Java, plays a central role here, and the breed is improved by the competitive bull races for which Madura is famous. Fishing, for which the Madurese use double-outrigger sailing canoes, is a major activity on the island. The Madurese are one of Indonesia's four main sea-faring peoples. Their cargo boats, which in former days brought cattle to East Java from as far away as Roti and Timor in Nusa Tenggara, are now used predominantly in the Sumatra timber industry.

The capital of the Republic, Jakarta, is in West Java, and it is in this sprawling city, where the ultramodern and extremely traditional meet head on, that the challenges of the future are first met. Jakarta is the cutting edge of change in Indonesia, exhibiting the benefits as well as the costs of rapid modernisation. There is great wealth, seen in the tree-lined avenues of the southern suburbs, and the abject poverty of the tarpaper slums on the edges of the city. Because people from all over the country meet here, bringing with them the food, clothing, language and customs of their different cultures, Jakarta can be seen as an Indonesia in microcosm.

Rahwana menacing Sita. Performed on the stage of the Prambanan complex not far from Yogyakarta, this splendid production of the Ramayana *tells the story of Rama, whose wife Sita is kidnapped by Rahwana, a rival king. The original epic was brought from India and translated over a thousand years ago. It was adapted for theatre in the 19th Century.*

OVERLEAF: *Looking as delicate as a Chinese brush painting, the town of Ngadisari wakes with the early morning sun. Its rays reflect off shiny surfaces — fish ponds and tin roofs.*

Although it is the custom all over the island of Java to refrain from public displays of emotion, after hours of formal ceremony this bride from Cigugur, West Java, shows her relief and happiness. The wedding party then moved to the area's only Catholic church for a short, second ceremony.

A Sundanese boy and his grandmother, from Cirebon, West Java.

Members of a musical troupe (above right) from Bandung. Their instruments, called angklung, *are made from differing lengths of bamboo. When shaken, each produces a different note. The* angklung, *an ancient instrument on Java and Bali, had fallen into disuse. It has recently been revived using Western scales and modern tunes.*

Nestling in a valley beside a steadily flowing stream is the village of Naga. Self sufficient in most respects, the people of this small community perfectly exhibit the Indonesian custom of gotong royong, mutual assistance.

If anyone has a need he or she cannot fulfil—anything from house repairs to extra food for a guest— the neighbours help, confident that they too will be helped in their time of need.

Women at a harvest festival, Cigugur, West Java.

In Cigugur, a few hours from Cirebon, the people annually give thanks for the season's harvest in a ceremony unique in the area. Processions of girls, boys, men and women start early in the morning to carry the harvest from four separate villages to a central temple atop a hill. A portion will be used for the ceremony and the rest stored in a granary near the temple. Also carried are elaborate offerings of fruit and woven leaves. Music and dancing, as always in Java, are an integral part of the ceremony.

59

Called Batavia by the Dutch, Jakarta, Indonesia's cpaital, is a bustling, cosmopolitan city. Traffic is always heavy on Jalan Thamrin, a wide modern boulevard crowded with hotels, office buildings and embassies.

Istana Merdeka, Freedom Palace, is the President's official residence. Jalan Gajah Mada, leading down to the harbour, is in the background.

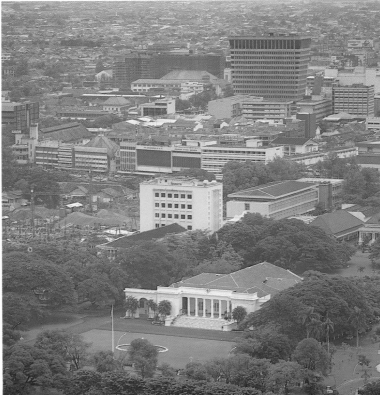

Jakarta's Istiqlal Mosque on the northeast corner of Merdeka Square is one of the world's largest mosques. The city's Roman Catholic cathedral stands close by.

The old port of Sunda Kelapa is the centre of inter-island trade in Jakarta. These elegant prahu pinisi sail all over Indonesia, bringing raw materials into Jakarta and supplying the islands with manufactured goods. Wide hulled and flat bottomed, with only a negligible projecting keel, they can carry an enormous amount of cargo. Although most are now equipped with engines, they generally follow monsoon winds as they sail around the islands.

61

Figures in a Chinese ancestral temple in Glodok, the city's original commercial centre. The man behind the desk selling oil and incense holders looks after the temple, where some of Jakarta's Chinese Indonesians come to pray.

Two Jakarta street scenes: Young poultry (above) for sale at Glodok market. In the background, the tattered remains of an election campaign poster. A row of becaks (right), Indonesia's omnipresent pedicabs, wait for fares outside a downtown hotel.

Indonesia produces some of the world's best badminton players. The game is incredibly popular, and children practise everywhere. This youngster, here using her front gate as a net, placed second in the all-Jakarta under-ten badminton competition.

63

Central Java is the heart of Indonesia's batik industry. Batik is made using a resist-dye process in which the design is waxed onto the cloth before it is dyed. Areas covered with wax do not take the dye, and after each dye bath the old wax is removed and different parts of the pattern waxed in. There are two kinds of batik, named for the way the wax is applied: In the finest examples, called batik tulis, designs are drawn by hand with a wax-filled canting or stylus. Batik cap is made with a copper stamp or print block, dipped in molten wax and· pressed onto the fabric. Although princes of the royal courts of Java often created designs for batik, the actual waxing of batik tulis is always carried out by women. Cap, on the other hand, is waxed by men. The finished product (left) is displayed at one of the many hotel fashion shows in Jakarta.

An actress (right) applies make-up before a performance. Small troupes throughout the island perform stories from the Hindu epics and Javanese history, as well as modern Javanese comic operas. These young people help ensure that traditional Javanese theatre remains a living part of Indonesian culture.

OVERLEAF: These two characters are Semar and Gareng, Java's ever-popular equivalent of Laurel and Hardy. They appear to a television audience of millions.

A performance of wayang kulit is a shadow play projected on a lamp-lit screen. The audience may sit on the shadow side or behind the dalang, watching him manipulate his flat leather puppets. Stories told in Javanese are usually from the Ramayana or Mahabharata, in a Javanese setting. Far more than just a puppeteer, the dalang, composes the dialogue and breathes life into the many puppets he controls, while directing the gamelan orchestra seated behind him.

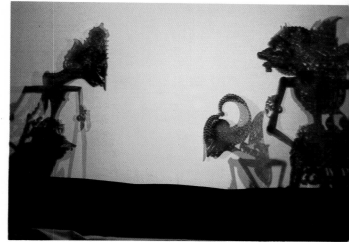

A puppet maker (above) bends and shapes the horn strips that support and move a wayang kulit. Made of goat skin or buffalo hide, the puppets are intricately carved and painted.

From the 7th to the 10th Century, Central Java was the site of intense temple-building activity under the Sailendra Dynasty. For reasons that are still a mystery, power moved to East Java. Temples long buried in earth and undergrowth disappeared from sight and memory. Prambanan (above) was once the god Shiva's principal temple in Java. One of eight restored Shivaite temples (left) on the Dieng Plateau. Built in the early 9th Century, they are among the oldest known Hindu temples in Java.

An uncovered Buddha gazes down from near the top of the Borobudur. This 9th-Century Buddhist hill temple, for centuries hidden by vegetation and volcanic ash, was only rediscovered in 1814. Villagers living nearby knew nothing of its existence except that it was a place of ill-omen. The Borobudur has been saved from collapse by a ten-year restoration programme under the auspices of UNESCO and the Indonesian Government.

A guard at the kraton, or Sultan's palace, in Yogyakarta. These proud quiet men, descendants of the old palace guard, lend dignity to one of Yogyakarta's main tourist attractions and are perhaps the most-often photographed figures in Indonesia. A world in time away, this Surabaya policeman conveys a totally different impression.

Thousands flock each year to a waterfall at Sedudo in the hills southwest of Surabaya. Bathing annually in its cool clear spray is said to cleanse the spirit. The festival begins with visitors from as far away as Jakarta immersing themselves in the waterfall and lasts as long as it takes everyone present to bathe. Pak Wo (top right) presides over Java's Fountain of Youth. When this photograph was taken, he was 103 years old.

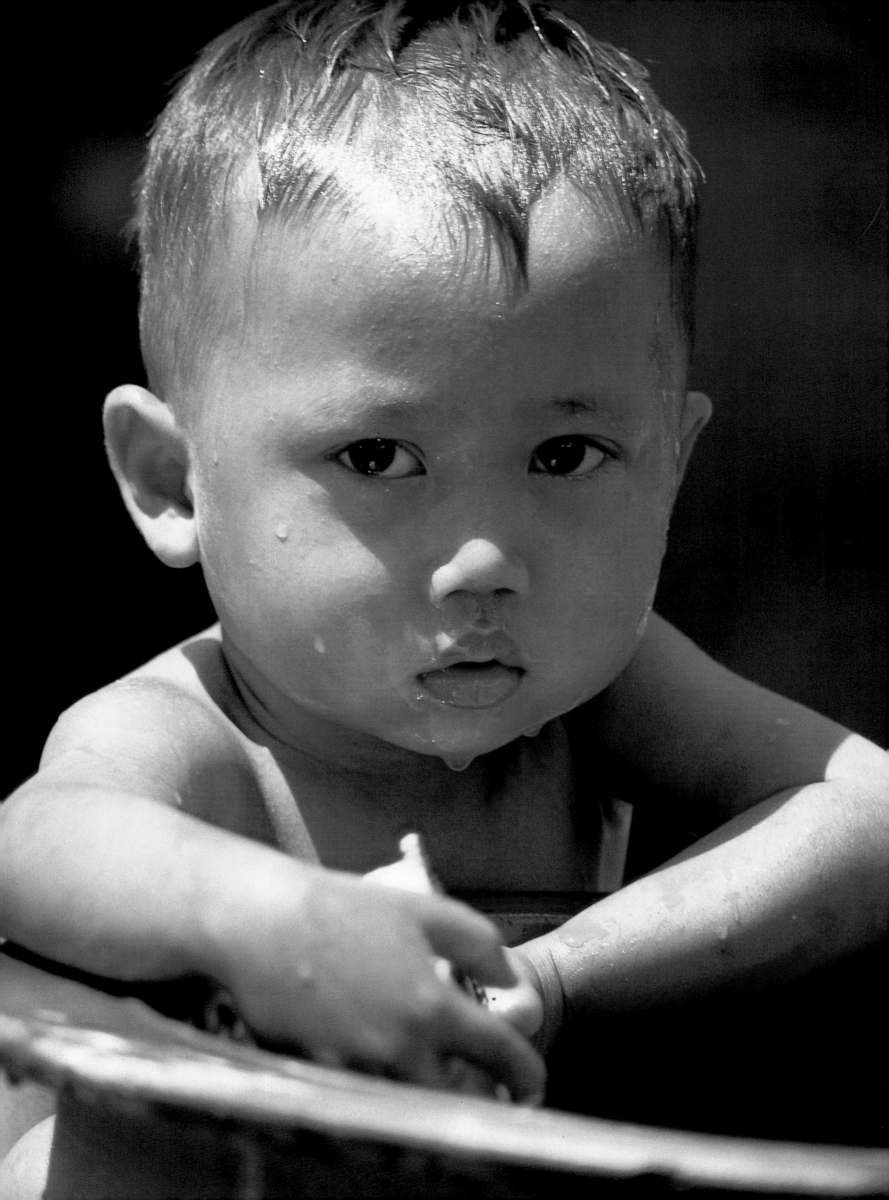

Bathing Indonesian style, this young boy uses a bucket to sluice down, then soaps all over and rinses again with water from the bucket.

The wife of the lurah or mayor of the Tengger village of Wonokitri. Although under Islam men are permitted four wives, the practice of polygamy in Indonesia has been severly curtailed under the 1974 marriage act. In this case, the lurah had been a widower for several years before marrying for the second time.

The mountains Batok in the foreground and Semeru in the distance both overshadow the rather unimpressive but better-known Mount Bromo to the left. One needs to stand on the lip and look into the depths of Bromo crater to feel the power that broods there. Accompanied by his hosts (right) at the unearthly hour of 4 a.m., the photographer views a spectacular sunrise over the mountain.

The area around Mt. Bromo is in many ways different from the rest of Java. The Tenggerese people practise their own religion, and some of their ceremonies are unique in Indonesia. In Wonokitri, for instance, one thousand days after the death of a village elder a ceremony takes place to release the spirit of the dead man. Called Entas-Entas, it starts with prayer and fasting. Small effigies, dressed in cloth once worn by the deceased, are then carried in a tower to the top of a sacred hill. Also carried, tied to the top of a pole, is the body of a bird, wings spread, whose soul will help the departed make the long journey. After chanting, and when the people are sure the spirit is ready, the effigies are slid down a chute and disrobed. The clothes are then cut up and placed in small coconut-shell bowls, doused in flammable liquid and set afire; shortly afterwards, the chute is also burned. The spirit is thus freed from all earthly ties and can leave in peace. A village elder later takes the effigies and burns them in private, scattering the ashes in a secret spot. Two young women (below right) watch the ceremony.

79

A Madurese woman on her way to market. Perhaps trading fish, she will buy rice, corn, vegetables and spices to supplement her family's fish diet.

The aquamarine seas at Telaga Biru in northwest Madura are cool, clear and refreshing. Not yet overwhelmed by tourists, the villagers are hospitable and friendly and show little interest in the hive of activity that exists in Surabaya, just a ferry ride away.

After a long night at sea the boats arrive at Ambunten (right) on the northeast coast of Madura. Nets are emptied and taken in to be washed, dried and repaired.

Not all men in the village go to sea. This village elder (left) tells tales common to fishermen everywhere.

Madura is famous for its bull races, held the first Sunday of every month. The races always start with dancing and a procession of beautifully decorated bulls in racing harness. Fed rice wine and whipped furiously during the race, the bulls are often hard to stop. These races are a source of great prestige to the breeders and their villages. Competition is fierce, and much care and preparation goes into the event. The second-place winner (right) proudly receives his prize.

83

The beaches on the dry south coast of Madura
are being stripped. These women take their
[...]

A lone farmer (right) works in his rice field near
Madura's south coast as the sun goes down.

Bali

Bali. The jewel at the eastern tip of Java, where the music of the *gamelan* fills the night, and gold-draped children dance the *legong*. A green, green island, where terraced hillsides meet the sky, and everyone is an artist.

The history of Bali has been turbulent, and in some of its episodes only slightly less fantastical than its legends. Ruled by Hindu Balinese kings from the earliest days of Hindu Java, the balance of power fluctuated between the two islands for a thousand years. Sometimes Bali was a vassal state, sometimes an independent kingdom. In the early 11th Century under Erlangga, the son of a Javanese princess and a Balinese prince, Bali even ruled Java for a time.

In 1343 General Gajah Mada of Java conquered Bali, and the island, along with the rest of the archipelago, became subject to Majapahit rule. The Kingdom fell during the reign of Brawijaya V when the ruler was told that in forty days the title of King of Majapahit would cease to exist. He took the prophecy so seriously that he burnt himself alive on the fortieth day. His son fled to Bali and proclaimed himself king. The rulers, priests, intellectuals and artists of the most civilised kingdom in Southeast Asia, along with the cream of Javanese culture, were transplanted in Bali's receptive soil. The art, religion and literature of Hindu Java were absorbed into Balinese culture and have flourished there, almost undisturbed, up to the present day.

In 1597 a fleet of Dutch ships discovered the island. For more than two hundred years the Dutch tried without success to gain control of Bali and her territories. In the mid-19th Century the first Dutch military expedition was sent to Bali over the issue of the ancient rights of the Balinese to salvage cargo from ships wrecked on her shores and by the late 1880's the Dutch had treaty rights with North Bali. By the beginning of the 20th Century they controlled all but the states in the south.

In 1904 a Chinese trading vessel, the *Sri Komala*, was wrecked and looted at Sanur on Bali's south coast. The owners applied for relief to the Dutch government, demanding three thousand silver dollars in damages from the Raja of Badung. After two years' negotiation, the Raja gave his final refusal, and a Dutch punitive expedition was launched against him. Five days later, when defeat was inevitable, the Raja gave his followers leave to return to their homes, inviting them, if they wished, to follow him to an honourable death. His advisors, priests, relations, wives, and many of his slaves and hereditary servants, all dressed in funeral white and carrying *kris* or short spears, prepared to accompany their lord into *puputan*, "the end". They marched in procession to meet the soldiers of the Royal Netherlands Indies Army, carrying the Raja on their shoulders under his gold umbrella of state. The women wore all their jewellery and

An actress takes a break back-stage during a performance of the Barong *dance.*

87

carried their babies. The Dutch commander begged them to stop, but they kept coming in a white and gold wave. At twenty metres they charged, waving their spears and *kris*. The Dutch had no choice but to fire. The Raja fell under the first volley, but his frenzied followers continued to attack. Men walked among the people, dispatching the wounded; priests sprinkled holy water on the dead and dying. The women of the palace threw their jewellery to the soldiers, stabbed their children and then themselves, falling in heaps over the body of the prince. When one group was killed another came to take its place until everyone was dead. The Dutch lost only one man.

Theirs was, however, a bitter victory that was to have tremendous consequences for the Balinese. The suicidal last stand of the royal house of Badung, although gaining them control over South Bali and the Rajas, was traumatic for the Dutch authorities. Not understanding what caused the Balinese to react so violently in the first place, they did not know what might cause them to react the same way again. Rather than risk a recurrence, the Dutch pursued a hands-off policy on Bali that was unprecedented in their handling of any other Indonesian possessions. The colonial administration was organised along much the same lines as it had been under the Rajas, and life went along virtually unchanged on the island.

In any case, the real life of Bali is in the hamlets and village temples and rice fields, not in the palaces of the great. A simple village in Bali is made of walled family courtyards lining tree-shaded streets. Where the two main streets intersect is the village square, and here are found the important public buildings. The village temple is here, as is the market, the cock-fight pavilion, the palace of the local lord if there is one, and the public assembly hall. There is also a tower where the *kulkul*, wooden slit-gongs used to summon the villagers to meetings or sound the alarm in times of trouble, are hung. Every village square also has its sacred *waringin* tree, under whose shadow many dances and village festivals take place. On the edges of the village are the cemetery and Temple of the Dead where the sacred guardian *barong* is kept, and in a cool shaded spot on the nearby river is the village bathing place.

Religion is a dominating force on Bali and pervades every aspect of life. Hinduism is practised on the island, but, mixed with animism

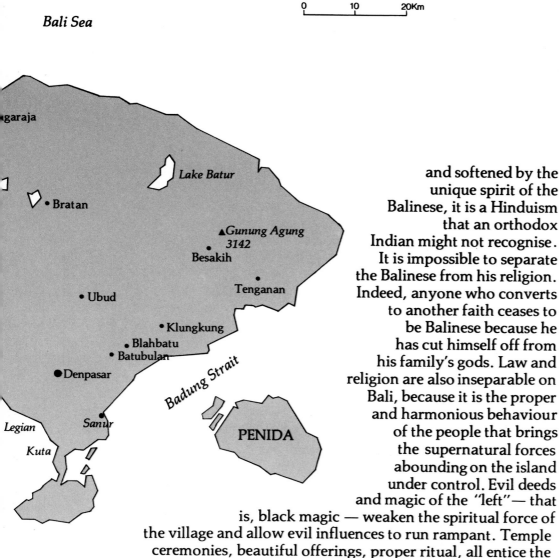

0   10   20Km

and softened by the unique spirit of the Balinese, it is a Hinduism that an orthodox Indian might not recognise. It is impossible to separate the Balinese from his religion. Indeed, anyone who converts to another faith ceases to be Balinese because he has cut himself off from his family's gods. Law and religion are also inseparable on Bali, because it is the proper and harmonious behaviour of the people that brings the supernatural forces abounding on the island under control. Evil deeds and magic of the "left" — that is, black magic — weaken the spiritual force of the village and allow evil influences to run rampant. Temple ceremonies, beautiful offerings, proper ritual, all entice the spirits of ancestors to stay in the village and keep it strong.

Balinese dance and drama are integral parts of religion, and performances are pleasing to the gods. Dancers are trained from the time they are tiny children and are highly valued in the community. A village which can train and support dancers of the *legong*, for instance, is exempt from taxes during the years they dance. Music is supplied by clubs of amateur musicians playing in *gamelan* orchestras. Those who can neither dance nor play may make the costumes or contribute in some other way. Rehearsals are long and arduous and usually take place at night, as do most performances. One wonders when the Balinese ever find the time to sleep.

The temple is the most important institution on Bali. Temples range from the grandeur of Bali's Mother Temple, Besakih, high on the slopes of the holy mountain Gunung Agung, to the small family shrines found in every household. Each household, in connection with the other families in their *banjar* or ward is responsible for its share of village temple maintenance and road building. The members of the *banjar* also pool resources for large temple ceremonies and musical activities. Families may also be members of the *subak*, which comprises all the households whose fields share the same irrigation source. The *subak* apportions the water to each family, guards the irrigation ditches and repairs the dikes.

The Balinese belongs to his family, his *banjar*, his *subak*, his temple and his village, living a communal and corporate life that has no counterpart in the West. But life is changing on Bali, as it is all over the developing world. As Indonesia's most important tourist attraction, this small island is inundated with thousands of visitors every year, and the resilient, unchanging Balinese culture is beginning to show the strain. The beaches—Sanur, Kuta, Legian—have lost their character and swarm with half-naked tourists and hawkers selling souvenirs and cheap clothing. Bus tours offer tourists the "real" Bali in half-day, whole-day, or two-day packages. There seems not to be a real Balinese in sight, and yet, through all the crush on Kuta's main street, a graceful youngster, ignoring the clamour, quietly sets out the evening offering of sticky rice and incense. Somewhere underneath all the noise and confusion the "real" Bali carries on.

Still, the problems of the outside world impinge on Bali too. Overpopulation is severe on this tiny island, and the overcrowding resulting from a high birthrate and long life make it, in the words of one old Balinese, "hard to breathe". Inflation also is taking its toll. People must work longer hours to meet the rising prices, and there is less time and money for traditional pursuits.

Tourism in Bali is a major foreign-exchange earner and is encouraged by the government. Bali alone attracts more visitors to Indonesia than all the other regions combined. Bali's unique culture and people are changing under the onslaught of foreign visitors. However, Bali has always been subject to foreign influences, and her people have been able to absorb what seemed useful, to change what did not quite fit, and to retain, in spite of everything, their own essential character.

A funeral procession on Kuta Beach. The bearers of these cremation bulls shout, chant and sing as they weave their way along Kuta's main street and turn down Jalan Pantai to the beach. The procession continues along the water's edge to the temple, where a mass cremation will be held. The remains of more than a hundred bodies were to be burned that day, many after waiting years for their families to collect enough money for the ceremony.

OVERLEAF: *Sunset over Tanahlot, a pagoda-like temple on a rock off the southwest coast.*

Time is computed in a special way on Bali, where a "year" has 210 days and a "week" can be anywhere from one to ten days long. The Balinese calender, in which these two cycles intersect, is based on the movements of the seven visible planets. Astrologers use the calender to cast horoscopes, and priests use it to fix the dates for ceremonies and festivals.

Once every Balinese year, each temple holds an *odalan* or anniversary festival. As there are hundreds of temples on the island, almost every day at least one ceremony is in progress somewhere. Here at Bukit Djambul the villagers spend the entire night at their temple, high on a hill overlooking Bali's east coast. These festivals ensure that the villagers do not lose contact with one another or with the village itself. Even those who have moved away to find work are expected to return for the ceremony.

Women wait beside their offerings for the ceremonies to begin. A Pemangku, or non-Brahman subsidiary priest (right), hands out woven-leaf offerings that have been blessed in the temple.

Small offerings like this one (right) are placed on the ground in front of houses, stores and temples all over Bali. Consisting of rice wine, water, rice, fruit, flower petals and incense, they are offered to appease evil spirits.

High on the slopes of Gunung Agung rests Besakih (below), Bali's mother temple. Called by Balinese the "navel of the world", every village on the island has a shrine here. Bits and pieces of this great temple are usually under repair, and the entire complex has been destroyed several times by natural disasters. Besakih's last and most dramatic levelling occurred in 1963 when Gunung Agung erupted during the Eka Dasa Rudra, a purification sacrifice which takes place only once every hundred years. It was the first time the holy mountain had erupted since the 14th Century. The ceremony was repeated in 1979.

95

Women (left) proudly carry offerings, piled high in silver bowls, to a temple ceremony. Traditionally made at home, there is a growing trend in the larger towns to buy them ready made. This is just one aspect of the changes occurring in Balinese religion in response to modern ideas and the pressure of increasing population.

After one 210-day Balinese year children have their first important contact with the religion and tradition that will guide them through the rest of their lives. Today this little girl will be named, blessed, and allowed to touch the ground for the first time. Three times, actually, once for each of the three deities that influence the lives of the Hindu-Balinese: Brahma, Shiva and Vishnu. The bowl in the foreground is used to bathe the child and to help the priestess at left to tell her future. She will be encouraged to pick up the various pieces of gold and silver jewellery in the water, each of which holds special meaning for her later years.

97

After a long life spent ministering to family and followers, a priestess is cremated at Blahbatu. Death is not an occasion for grief on Bali, but rather the joyous beginning of the soul's great journey to another life. The tower, representing the cosmos, dips and weaves its way to the cremation site, carrying the corpse high above the crowds of villagers, tourists and followers gathered to pay last respects or simply to watch. The bearers are all family or former students of the priestess.

On the way from the family's gate to the cremation site, the tower is turned three times to confuse evil spirits and prevent the soul of the deceased from trying to return to her former home. Having arrived at the nearby field, the corpse is swiftly transferred to a bull-shaped coffin, mantras are chanted, and the fire starts. Both the bull and tower are yellow and white, the colours of the Brahman caste.

As the heat intensifies, cleansing the bones and incinerating the bull, the arm joints contract, causing the arms slowly and eerily to rise. Later the remaining few bones will be crushed and ground, mixed with cane sugar, and ceremonially spread along the nearby shore.

A woman from Tenganan, East Bali, explains the ancient art of weaving grinsing, *the sacred Balinese double-* ikat *textile.* Grinsing, *which has the power to protect the wearer from illness and evil, is an important part of many ceremonies on Bali and is woven only in this village. An incredibly complex process, it involves dying the pattern into both the warp and weft threads, and, because various components of the dyes can only be gathered during certain phases of the moon, it can take as long as nine years to dye and weave a single piece of* grinsing *. The Indonesian government considers* grinsing *a national treasure; it may not be taken out of the country.*

Villagers work in the drained rice fields at harvest time. Threshing the rice stalks frees the grains from the stalk; the grain will later be pounded to separate the husk from the inner kernel. Rice that is consumed locally is husked a little at a time, only enough for one day's cooking. Green rice terraces (below) are a popular image in Balinese paintings.

With bemused expressions on their faces, these muttering, tripping ducks head for home. They spend their days lazing, bathing and growing, never straying from the pole of their owner who returns late every afternoon to take them home. Their lives are a short six months, as they are destined for temple offerings or family ceremonies.

103

Three dancers rest onstage while the main action continues elsewhere. Balinese dance-dramas are justly famous all over the world.

A seven-year-old girl (below) performs the Sanghyang trance dance. She has dressed and put on her make-up with little help from others and is put into trance by a priest before being conducted to the stage. As the chorus begins to sing and chant, the girls begin to dance. Although never taught to dance, no one is surprised at their skill; their bodies are occupied by the spirits of female deities who dance for them.

Bells, drums, metallaphones and gongs make up the Balinese gamelan orchestra used here to set the various moods of a Barong dance at Batubulan.

The young man (above) is one of the Barong's followers.

The Barong dance enacts the struggle between the forces of harmony and discord, climaxing with a fight between the Barong (right), a mythical creature whose magic power is concentrated in his beard, and the witch Rangda (below).

The fight is inconclusive, and the Barong leaves the stage to summon his followers. They attack Rangda, but she rallies and casts a spell, causing them to turn their knives upon themselves. The witch departs in glee, but the young men are protected by the Barong's magic, and the blades do not harm them. They are released from trance by the Barong and a Pemangku.

A group of children take a break from selling souvenirs and fly their kite on Legian beach. Nearby a sun-loving tourist relaxes on the hot sand. The woman to her right, carefully protected from the sun, waits to give her a massage.

A village scene comes to life under the hand of one of Bali's many painters. Bali's long tradition of artistic expression provides fertile ground for her many budding artists.

Silverware, necessary for all ceremonies in one form or another, is finely worked and of high quality. Samples from this village suburb of Singaraja, capital of North Bali, include bowls, cups and other containers. Although jewellery and objects of modern design are making their way into tourists' hands, most of this craftman's work will eventually be used in ceremonies by people from surrounding villages.

Wood carving (far right) is a treasured craft on the island. This rendition of Vishnu riding on Garuda is a fine example of the traditional Balinese style.

107

A girl receiving blessings at a temple ceremony.

Sitting in one of the open houses in the public meeting area, an afternoon is spent making a new cage for a prized fighting cock.

Kalimantan

Kalimantan. The Indonesian two-thirds of Borneo, one of the largest and most mysterious islands in the world. Its dense, often impenetrable forests abound with wildlife, many species of which are not found anywhere else in the world. The deep waters of the Mahakam river, for instance, harbour a rare species of freshwater dolphin. There are clouded leopards, hundreds of species of exotic birds, reptiles, and insects, and a bewildering variety of monkeys and apes, including the rare proboscis monkey and the orangutan. The most important creature of the forest, from a symbolic point of view, is the black hornbill, soul carrier of the Dayaks. Since prehistoric times the hornbill has played a major role in Dayak culture, but, hunted for its feathers and huge beak, the hornbill was in danger of extinction. Now a protected species, its numbers are increasing. The durian, Southeast Asia's notorious "smelly fruit", flourishes in the jungles, and Kalimantan's durian *lai* is considered the most delicious of all varieties. Durian smells like a combination of sour milk, onions and over-ripe mangoes. It tastes, to those who appreciate its flavour, like heaven; to those who don't, durian tastes the way it smells.

Although its area is huge, the population is sparse, and the island's incredibly rough terrain makes communication and travel difficult. Life in Kalimantan centres on the many rivers that serve as the main channels of communication throughout the island. Roads are few, and where there are no navigable rivers travel is virtually impossible.

Like Sumatra and Java, the island was a cultural crossroad in prehistoric and early historic times. In the Neolithic period, migrants moving south from China brought with them artifacts and technology from the Chou Dynasty and the Sino-Vietnamese Dongson culture that has been influential all over western Indonesia. Sanskrit inscriptions dating from around 400 A.D. give evidence of Hindu influence in East Kalimantan, and it is likely that the area was a trade centre on the much-travelled route between China, the Philippines, and the Javanese Majapahit Kingdom. Many bronzes and porcelains in the style of the Chou Dynasty have been found in Kalimantan, and in inland areas Chinese-style bronze gongs are important items of currency, used especially to pay the bride price when a couple marries.

There are three basic ethnic groupings in Kalimantan: coastal Malays, relatively recent arrivals who follow Islam and live in towns and cities and small settlements at the mouths of the rivers; ethnic Chinese, who have controlled trade in Kalimantan for centuries; and the island's original inhabitants, the Dayaks. Dayak is a comprehensive term used to describe more than two hundred inland tribal groups. Originally coastal dwellers, they have been driven farther and farther inland by successive migrations of Malays. They

A Dayak from Tanjung Manis, East Kalimantan. Ear piercing is a common practice among men and women in Kalimantan. Lobes are pierced to hold ornaments, but the holes in the upper part of the ear once held boar's or leopard's teeth.

111

inhabit the river
banks and highlands
deep in the jungle and
live a life not very different
from that of their
Neolithic forebears.
Dayak culture varies
from tribe to tribe, but
most of it centres around
the *lamin* or longhouse.
A Dayak village may
consist of one large
lamin — some in
East Kalimantan are nearly
300 metres long—or several
smaller ones. *Lamin* are built on
ironwood piles often three metres
high to offer protection from
enemies, wild animals and
flooding. Notched ironwood logs,
sometimes beautifully carved, serve as
ladders which can be pulled up into the
longhouse at need.

Pontianak

R. Kapuas

Anji

Java Sea

The area below the house is used to stable domestic animals, usually pigs and chickens. Above, longhouses are divided lengthwise. Most have a communal verandah running the length of one side and private family quarters running the length of the other side. In some groups, however, private quarters line both sides of a central verandah. The verandah is the main street and communal area of the *lamin*. Here the women pound the rice and mend the fishing nets. Villagers meet here, and here the traditional, songs, dances and ceremonies are performed. In one Dayak group there is a sunken square built on springy poles in the middle of the verandah. It is used for jumping dances, and acts much like a trampoline. Fish traps, paddles, blowpipes and clothing are stored on the verandah, and the unmarried men sleep there. The space under the roof is used to store rice, baskets, mats, fishing nets and other valuables.

Until quite recently head-hunting was an important activity among many Dayak tribes. Heads were needed to keep a village strong and for ceremonial functions, such as the building of a new *lamin*. They were useful in warding off plague and famine and in keeping evil spirits at bay. The continual threat of head-hunting raids from neighbouring villages turned longhouses into well-fortified bastions of defense. In some places, the verandahs were made of loosely-tied lengths of bamboo which rattle when walked upon, to

Map labels:

Tarakan

Sulawesi Sea

0 50 100Km

▲ *Mt Menyapa* 2000

R. Boh

•Long Segar
•Long Noran
•Long Wai

R. Wahau

kam

Equator

R. Mahakam
•Samarinda

•Balikpapan

•Tanjung

Makassar Strait

ung
R. Barito

Banjarmasin
•Martapura

warn of night-time intruders looking for heads.

Dayaks practise slash-and-burn farming, growing rice, corn, yams, pumpkin and cucumber. In inland areas where the soil is peaty and not particularly fertile, the fields quickly become exhausted. Entire villages are often abandoned as the available fertile land declines. Some Dayak groups take their *lamin* with them when they move. Fitted together without the use of nails, the houses are disassembled and moved to the new village site. Each family owns and is responsible for the timber comprising its private living area and the part of the verandah directly outside its door.

The Dayaks do not live by agriculture alone; fishing, hunting and gathering all play a part in the subsistence economy of these people. In the last thirty years or so, the use of metal tools has become common; historically, however, the Dayaks have used polished stone tools. Many of the ancient crafts persist. Although some groups practise weaving, and textiles from Java and other islands are easily obtainable in Kalimantan, bark-cloth is still made and used here. Baskets and mats, finely woven in designs from the late Chou period, are offered for sale in local and off-island markets. Dayak beadwood is excellent. Some of the beads still in circulation came to Kalimantan from Italy in the time of Marco Polo.

Not all Dayaks live in settled villages. One group, the Punan, live in a much more primitive style than their relatively sophisticated neighbours. They are classic hunters and gatherers and wander through the forests at will. Although the government is encouraging them to live in villages and cultivate rice, most Punan are not interested in settling down. They may live in a village for a few weeks or even months, but the houses are often abandoned in the pursuit of their traditional nomadic ways.

Kalimantan has greatly changed since the turn of the century, especially in the last forty years or so, and much the old Dayak culture has gone or is fast disappearing. Head-hunting, as elsewhere in Indonesia, is a thing of the past. Ceremonial life is in decline, and the rule of *adat*, tradition, has been broken by the conversion of many Dayaks to either Christianity or Islam. *Tuak*, a kind of palm wine drunk at many ceremonies and dances, has been forbidden by the

113

Protestant missionaries; without it, the ceremonies and dances do not take place. Longhouse living has been discouraged both by missionaries and by the Indonesian government on the grounds that it is unsanitary and spreads disease. Conventional Javanese-style villages are replacing them, but the longhouse-centred communal Dayak culture does not survive in these villages.

Timber is big business in Kalimantan, and the island's wealth of natural hardwoods is proving to be a mixed blessing. Indiscriminate tree-felling has led to serious erosion in some areas, and, although reforestation projects have been undertaken, it will take decades to repair the damage. Timbering has also disturbed the breeding patterns and destroyed the habitat of many species of wildlife already rare in the world's forests. The government has lately taken steps to restrict timbering and protect the forests and their inhabitants, but poaching of both trees and animals is easy and, given the size of the jungle, almost impossible to prevent.

In the vicinity of Balikpapan, locally known as *Kota Minyak* or "Oil City", is an immense field of natural gas. Thousands of foreigners and Indonesians from other islands have come to work in Balikpapan and nearby Badak, where a huge liquefaction plant has been built. The contrast between the lives of these outsiders and the local inhabitants is staggering. The influx of coastal peoples and traders upriver has had an eroding effect on Dayak culture. As always, when faced with pressure from outside, the Dayaks retreat farther inland to parts of Kalimantan as yet inaccessible to outsiders.

The Dayaks are, of course, only one part of Kalimantan's story. The coastal people and those who live in the increasingly modern and prosperous cities and towns are more in the mainstream of Indonesian life than they have been since the great days of the Majapahit Empire. People flock to Kalimantan from all over Indonesia, especially Java, looking for work, and the modern world is fast encroaching on the jungle. Although the days of the "wild man of Borneo" are fading fast, the jungles of Kalimantan are still the custodians of precious cultural and natural treasures.

A man and woman chat at a floating market in Banjarmasin on the Barito River, South Kalimantan. The market consists of a group of boats, large and small, to which buyers and sellers come in their simple dugout canoes. Trading begins soon after sunrise and lasts until mid-morning. At nine or ten o'clock people begin their journeys home, disappearing up the many small tributaries of the river.

OVERLEAF: *A father and son fish for prawns on the Mahakam River, East Kalimantan. Some of the rattan baskets on board are used to trap the shellfish; others are used to store the catch.*

114

A woman bathes her child on one of her village's several floating *tempat mandi*. These platforms tied to the bank serve as wash-houses, jetties, entrances to the village and gathering places for the village women.

Like children everywhere, the young in Kalimantan are quick to invent games in their spare time. Stilts, hopscotch and bicycle riding are popular, and in the hot weather a quick plunge in the river is always welcome.

A Kenyah Dayak woman cheerfully mixes the old and new. Wearing Western clothes and smoking a cigarette, she also bears the traditional tatoos of a Dayak lady. Her earlobes, though pierced to hold heavy gold or brass rings, are modern and empty.

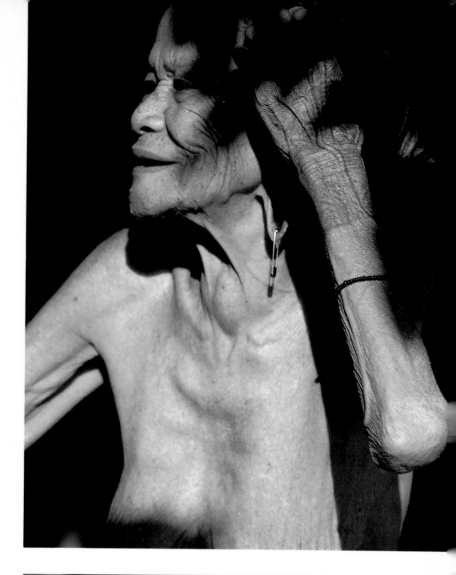

An old woman (right), quietly watching the world go by from her house on the river, has decorated one lobe with a safety pin. Almost a hundred years old, she has seen enormous changes since the days when she and her family wandered deep in the forests. The tatoos on her forearms and calves, intricate curvilinear designs of birds and spirits, are a legacy of the time when all Dayak women thought them beautiful and necessary.

The village head of Neheslah Bing on the Mahakam River. A Modang Dayak, his ears are pierced for ornaments only. Had be been a headhunter in bygone days, his upper ears would have been pierced to display trophies.

The rain forests are the home of many primates, including macaque monkeys (left), proboscis monkeys (above) and orangutans like Rico (right), an adolescent male seen here prowling around the orangutan rehabilitation centre in Tanjung Puting, a wildlife reserve in Central Kalimantan. This centre helps orangutans which have been kept as pets return to their native forests. Orangutans are a protected species in Indonesia, but their future is still at risk. Although the indiscriminate deforestation which destroyed huge areas of their habitat has ended, the controlled timbering which continues is enough to disrupt their breeding patterns. Orangutans are shy creatures, easily frightened, and when under stress their fertility rate drops drastically. Sumatra and Borneo are the only places in the world where these rare primates can be found. If the areas where they can live undisturbed continue to shrink, they could face extinction in the wild.

Cocks in a training fight in Central Kalimantan. In real matches they wear poisoned spurs, and death occurs within seconds after a wound is inflicted.

In many parts of Indonesia, babies are carried in selendangs, long strips of fabric looped under one arm and fastened on the opposite shoulder. Dayak babies, however, ride in beautifully decorated wooden or rattan carriers on their mothers' chests or backs. Baby carriers may be painted, beaded, carved or hung with coins, ribbons and pieces of ivory. The coloured ones are most commonly black with yellow designs, as are the two shown here. The Dayaks are famous for their beadwork, and many of the glass beads still in circulation are Italian, having come to Kalimantan from China in the time of Marco Polo.

The Kenyah Dayaks are splendid dancers. This swift and skillful mock attack (far right) is performed with traditional Dayak swords called mandau. The mandau is as important to the Dayaks as the Kris is to the Javanese, and as much care goes into its making. The carved handles (right) are especially beautiful. Unlike Kris, which can only be used in battle or ritual, mandau are often put to practical use.

The central pole in the meeting house at Long Noran, East Kalimantan. Interpretations vary, but the village chief tells of an ancient king and the burung enggang or black hornbill, soul-carrier of the dead. These as well as flowing water, mandau and other symbols can clearly be seen on the pole. There is also a martavan, a Chinese storage vessel made of porcelain or earthenware decorated with dragons and floral designs. Many martavan are truly old, dating back to the Ming Dynasty, but their desirability as collectors' pieces has led to a flourishing trade in forgeries.

Kalimantan is mainly jungle,
penetrated by numerous rivers
which are the main lines of
communication on the island.
Small outboard and inboard
engines are being used more and
more, but dugouts, paddled with
the single carved Dayak oar, are
still a common sight. Thick
vegetation cloaks both sides of the
river, broken only by occasional
houses and timber concessions.

A man empties a sack of rice (left)
onto a woven mat. The flower
tatoos on his shoulders and chest
identify him as Punan, one of the
original inhabitants of the island
whose ancesters moved inland as
waves of migration forced them
away from the coast. Like the Kubu
of South Sumatra, the Punan are
nomadic hunters and gatherers,
roaming the forests of East
Kalimantan. Occasional contact
with river dwellers has brought
with it stories of the outside world,
and with encouragement from the
government, some Punan are
beginning to live a more settled life.

The Dayaks practise dry-rice cultivation, rather than the wet-field method practised in Java and Bali. These fields, called ladang, are in Long Segar, East Kalimantan. This family works for a few hours each morning, and then everyone settles down for the mid-morning meal. They return to the village by noon to rest and prepare the evening meal of rice, vegetables and the occasional fish.

127

In a village on the upper reaches of the Mahakam river, a woman weaves a fishing net on the verandah of her lamin *or longhouse.*

In any small village a death in the community is a major event and a time of mourning for all. In this new Punan village, comprised exclusively of one large extended family, the dead woman (above) was the oldest member to arrive at this isolated shallow tributary of the Mahakam river; now she is the first to leave it.

South Kalimantan is one of Indonesia's major diamond-producing provinces. A large variety of precious and semi-precious stones find their way from mines here to market places around the country. Jakarta in particular has a number of markets frequented by shabby-looking but eloquent salesmen who tell of magic gems from mines in distant Kalimantan. The mines themselves, however, silt-filled waterlogged holes and pits dug along the mouths of ancient streams, are not nearly so romantic. A miner, up to his waist in water, works at a diamond mine near Martapura.

At Tanjung market a woman sells dried fish, a dietary staple all over Indonesia.

130

South and East Kalimantan are famous through Indonesia for their high-quality mat and basket weaving. Intricately designed, they are prized for their beauty as well as for durability and strength.

131

Early morning on the Barito River, near Banjarmasin, South Kalimantan.

A young girl from Anjir Serapat (right), a small village in South Kalimantan, is being dressed for her most untraditional-looking wedding. Wearing a curled black wig and a white dress with a Paris label, she awaits the arrival of the groom from a village down river. One hundred and eighty guests were present to witness the formal meeting of the young couple. The bride was third in her family to wear this spectacular outfit, which is at least two generations old. Nearly as elegant as she, the groom wore a black and grey pinstriped suit.

Sulawesi

Sulawesi. An odd orchid-shaped island in the middle of Indonesia, with three long petals topped by a curving stem. Each peninsula is ridged with central mountains and surrounded by coral reefs. The northernmost part of the island was once linked to the Philippines. When the land bridge was broken, many plants and animals were isolated and the island evolved into a zone of wildlife unique in Indonesia. Sulawesi is the home of the *babi rusa*, a pig-like animal with curving tusks; the *anoa*, a fierce pygmy buffalo living in the mountains of the north central part of the island; and the black-crested baboon. Away from the coastal fringe, the land is covered with rain forests and rugged unarable highlands.

In prehistoric times, from about 12,000 to 4,000 years ago, Sulawesi was an entrepot for many races and cultures. As new waves of migration moved onto the coasts, the older inhabitants moved inland. The mountainous interior makes communication and travel difficult. Rivers are narrow and for the most part unnavigable, and until the Spanish brought horses in the 17th Century, the only mode of transportation inland was on foot. Communities out of reach of the sea had to be self sufficient if they were to survive. The resulting pattern of inland settlement was one of isolated ethnic groups with very different cultural patterns, until recently having little contact with each other or the outside world. The largest and perhaps oldest of these groups is the Toraja, the people of the mountains. Tana Toraja (Torajaland) is located in the centre of the orchid, in an area that comprises parts of the provinces of Central and South Sulawesi. Until Christian missionaries entered their lands in the early 19th Century, the Toraja lived in almost total seclusion from the foreign influences that had been flooding coastal Sulawesi for hundreds of years. All outside trade occured through the mediation of the Bajau sea nomads from northeast Kalimantan who were the only people the Toraja would tolerate. Now, however, because of the uniqueness of the culture and its interest for tourists, the number of outsiders passing through the area every year has dramatically increased.

The first thing that strikes a visitor to Tana Toraja are the houses. A traditional Toraja house or *tongkonan*, is built according to unchanging ancient requirements. It must stand facing north, the source of felicity, and its entrance must face the east, which is associated with life. Built without nails and sitting on top of thick octagonal posts, it must be made in such a way that it can be moved without falling apart. Rice barns, smaller versions of the *tongkonan*, are built in a row in front of the house. The number of barns indicates the wealth of the family. Only women may enter the upper part of the barn where the rice is stored. Underneath is an open platform where guests are received. The most striking feature of the house is its sweeping boat-shaped roof, thatched with split bamboo.

A guest at a death feast in Tana Toraja, South Sulawesi.

The strong central pillar in front of the house is usually decorated with buffalo horns, each set of horns representing a death feast the family has given. The more horns, the higher the status of the family.

Toraja houses not only look like boats, in an important symbolic way they are boats. Some of the rooms are even named after a boat's major parts. The south room is the captain's bridge; the central room is the midships and contains the central post of the house, rising like a mast, where the family heirlooms are stored. There is also a room for grandparents and guests, and a verandah running the length of the north side of the house. Walls are engraved and painted with symmetrical designs in yellow, red and white.

Death is an important part of Toraja life, perhaps the most important, and the area is known for its elaborate funeral feasts. Today many Toraja are Christian, but the beliefs and rituals of *Aluk To'dolo*, the old religion, still persist. Funerals are expensive, but the average Torajan considers the ceremony to be the most important event in his life. The government, in an attempt to reduce the amount of money spent this way, has limited the number of beasts that may be sacrificed. Because a person's comfort and status in the next world is measured by the splendour of his funeral, this rule is impossible to enforce. By the time many buffaloes and pigs have been slaughtered and all the guests provided with food, shelter and entertainment for several weeks, a family's carefully hoarded wealth can be wiped out. Often it takes time to collect enough money for a death feast, and the corpse sometimes waits years before burial is possible. During the interim the deceased is thought to be "ill". He or she is visited daily, offered food and cigarettes, and treated with great love and respect.

A death feast in Tana Toraja only lasts a few days, but it cannot begin until all the relatives have assembled. There is often a wait of several weeks before everyone has arrived. When everything is ready, the coffin is carried in procession to the *rante*, a field where tall stones stand. Special houses, called *lantang*, have been built there for the relatives of the deceased, as well as a special pavilion where the coffin lies in state. As soon as the coffin has been placed in the pavilion, buffalo fights are held. The second day is a day of rest. On the third day, groups of guests enter the *rante*, proceeded by their gifts of buffalo, pigs and palm wine. They file past all the *lantang* and are finally

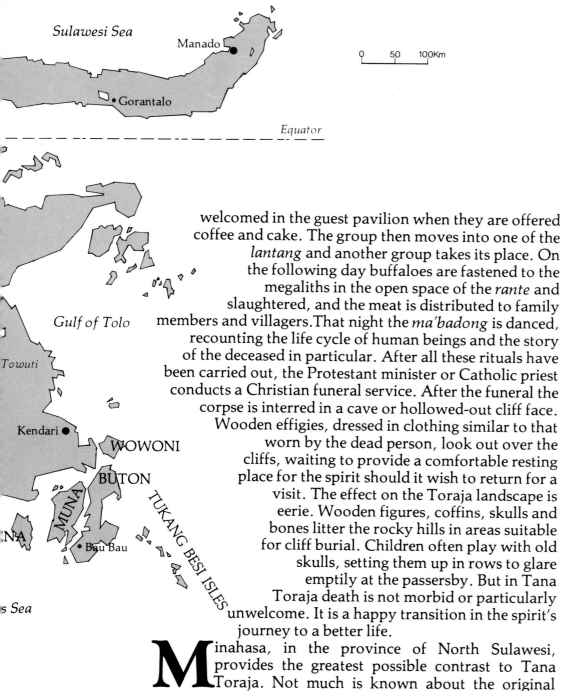

Sulawesi Sea

Manado

0   50   100Km

Gorantalo

Equator

Gulf of Tolo

Towuti

Kendari

WOWONI

BUTON

MUNA

NA

Bau Bau

TUKANG BESI ISLES

s Sea

welcomed in the guest pavilion when they are offered coffee and cake. The group then moves into one of the *lantang* and another group takes its place. On the following day buffaloes are fastened to the megaliths in the open space of the *rante* and slaughtered, and the meat is distributed to family members and villagers. That night the *ma'badong* is danced, recounting the life cycle of human beings and the story of the deceased in particular. After all these rituals have been carried out, the Protestant minister or Catholic priest conducts a Christian funeral service. After the funeral the corpse is interred in a cave or hollowed-out cliff face. Wooden effigies, dressed in clothing similar to that worn by the dead person, look out over the cliffs, waiting to provide a comfortable resting place for the spirit should it wish to return for a visit. The effect on the Toraja landscape is eerie. Wooden figures, coffins, skulls and bones litter the rocky hills in areas suitable for cliff burial. Children often play with old skulls, setting them up in rows to glare emptily at the passersby. But in Tana Toraja death is not morbid or particularly unwelcome. It is a happy transition in the spirit's journey to a better life.

Minahasa, in the province of North Sulawesi, provides the greatest possible contrast to Tana Toraja. Not much is known about the original Minahasa culture because North Sulawesi, with its capital city of Manado, came under such strong European influence in the 17th Century that most indigenous traditions were lost. Most Minahasans are Christian as a result of education in Dutch mission schools, and Western dress is common throughout the area.

The most important crop is cloves, used to make *kretek*, Indonesian cigarettes. North Sulawesi is also Indonesia's biggest producer of copra, or dried coconut kernels, and every family seems to have at least a small stand of coconut palms. The Minahasa people are great traders, and the per capita income in this area is one of the highest in the entire country.

South Sulawesi is also a relatively wealthy area. For years it was the Dutch rice granary, supplying possessions in Maluku. The provincial capital, Ujung Pandang (formerly called Makassar), is the major trading port. Ujung Pandang is the home of the Makassar people, who, with the Bugis of the east coast of the peninsula, form the major ethnic groups in South Sulawesi.

Many Makassarese make their living on the sea. They, along with the Bugis people, are among the most influential of the sea-faring groups of Indonesia. Once feared throughout Asian waters as their pirate ships preyed on weaker vessels, these two groups dominate Indonesia's inter-island trade. For thousands of years they have followed the monsoons in their black-sailed *prahu*, trading sophisticated consumer goods from the cities for jungle products, raw materials and delicacies from the sea. The Bugis and Makassarese traditionally voyaged north to the Philippines and eastward to the Kai and Aru islands to collect sandalwood, mother-of-pearl, bird nests, shark fins, and plumes from the bird of paradise, all for the Chinese market. *Trepang*, or sea cucumber, was also an important item, and Bugis *prahu* went as far as the northwest coast of Australia to find it. They also traded with the Australian Aborigines for tortoise shell. Today they dominate the timber and general cargo trade on the Surabaya–Banjarmasin and the Surabaya–Ujung Pandang routes. Their boats have scarcely changed in centuries. Although they now use diesel engines and are built with iron nails, the two tall masts still carry huge areas of canvas. And, as they have always done, they sail without insurance, loaded to the plimsoll line with everything from rice and onions to motor-cycles and bicycle tyres for the outer islands of the archipelago.

A chorus of singers on Tomea Island, Southeast Sulawesi, wait for the dancing to begin.

OVERLEAF: *Boats on a beach west of Manado, North Sulawesi. They are covered with leaves to protect them from the sun.*

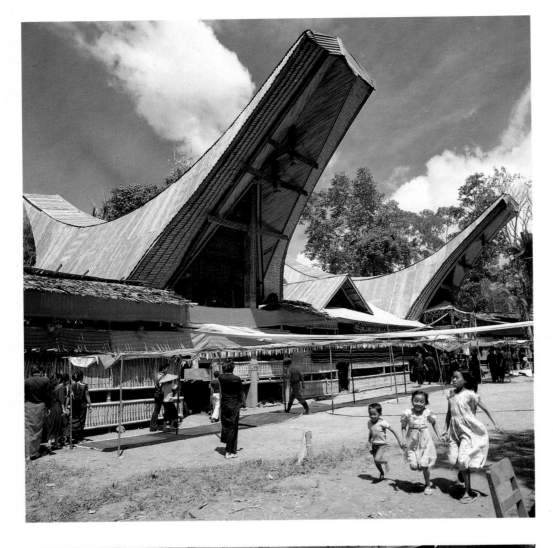

Toraja houses are typically boat shaped, with sweeping roofs. Buffalo horns, symbols of prosperity, often grace the gables and entrances. As is the case with traditional houses all over Indonesia, corrugated iron roofs are fast replacing the cooler and more serviceable thatch. Awnings have been set up in front of the verandahs to accommodate guests at a death feast.

A group of men play cards in the shade under the house while waiting for festivities to begin.

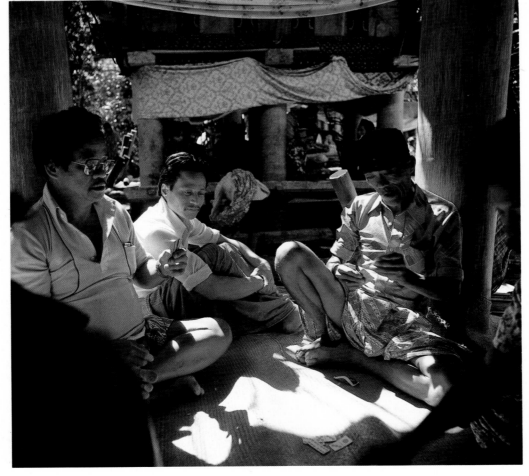

142

As brightly dressed girls sing and chant a welcome,
guests arrive in procession to be greeted by family
members of the deceased. Women hosts greet lines of
women guests, offer betel nut, and show them to their
seats. Men are similarly greeted, but with cigarettes
instead of betel.

For the Toraja, the "people of the mountains" of south
Central Sulawesi, death is a happy state. A corpse is
given two feasts: one shortly after death, and a second
some time later when conditions are right and the
family has accumulated the wealth it needs to perform
the ceremony properly. The time between a person's
death and final burial he or she is said to be "ill".
Great care is taken to keep the corpse comfortable and
happy, and family members take turns keeping it
company so the soul will not be lonely.

A funeral is both a solemn and a joyous occasion, as it signals the soul's release from the body and the beginning of its journey to another life. But funerals can be staggeringly expensive. A person's stature is measured in terms of the size and grandeur of his funeral, and wealth accumulated during a lifetime of hard work is often dissipated at this time. Many animals, especially buffaloes and pigs, are slaughtered and distributed to the guests. It is customary for friends and neighbours to contribute food or animals, and a careful tally is kept. The contributions are reciprocated and sometimes increased when someone in the donor's family dies. Guests watch with interest as this magnificent bull is slaughtered and cut up for distribution.

145

While waiting for burial, the corpse, drained of fluids, has spent the interim in the house of his family or in a temporary grave nearby. Should the wait be long, the bones will be exhumed and cleaned; otherwise the body will remain in the casket until after the feast when it is taken to its resting place high in a rock cliff. For poorer families any large rock will do, even one by the side of the road.

A wall of tombs (left) looms eerily at Lemo Lemo, near Rantepao in South Sulawesi. The figures looking out from ledges in the rock are about a metre tall and wear clothing similar to that once worn by the deceased. Should any of the dead wish to come back for a look at the world they have left behind, he or she will have the use of eyes and a well-dressed body.

Figures and rotting coffins (left below) where a rock face, honey-combed with graves, has collapsed. The cult of death is so pervasive in Tana Toraja that the landscape seems, at times, to be fairly littered with skulls. This row was probably set up by local children as a joke.

The province of North Sulawesi is as different from Tana Toraja as can be imagined. Strongly influenced by Western traders and missionaries from as early as the 16th Century, the indigenous Minahasa culture has virtually disappeared. This man, with his sparkling white shirt and well-worn hat, is from the mountain town of Tomohon, near Manado.

146

These small Minahasa villages are amazingly prosperous. Heavily wooded areas give way to wide suburban streets lined with brick and tile houses. North Sulawesi is one of Indonesia's wealthiest provinces, and its wealth comes from cloves. All the cloves grown here are used in the manufacture of kretek cigarettes, more than 50 million of which are produced and smoked every year. Cloves are picked by hand and dried in the sun. Few people have gardens in clove-growing country. Every available square inch of flat ground is covered with concrete and used to dry the crop.

Minahasa food can be quite exotic. Dry-roasted rats (top right) are considered a delicacy.

A hazy Makassar landscape, western South Sulawesi.

The Bugis and Makassarese people live in peninsular South Sulawesi. Bugis communities are mainly on the east coast while the Makassarese live on the west. These people loom large in legend, and it is thought that the terrifying "bogey man", whose name alone frightened generations of children into good behaviour, started his career as a Bugis pirate.

The Bugis and Makassarese also have a reputation for being some of the harshest people in Indonesia, and those encountered on the mainland do not seem greatly enamoured of foreigners. On the islands southeast of the peninsula, however, people are softer and more amenable to strangers. A Bugis woman from the island of Kalao Toa looks into the camera, her head modestly covered with a towel. Another flashes a shy gold-toothed smile.

Bugis traders are famous throughout Indonesia as boat-builders, sailors and pirates, and ships feature in all aspects of life. The roof ornament (top left) is a copy of the carved prow of a Bugis sailing ship. A villager (above) hitches a ride as he stands beside his banana-filled canoe. Friendly and hospitable, the people of this little island show none of the fearsome aggression that gave Bugis sailors the title "Scourge of the Java Seas".

151

The Bugis village on Kalao Toa is built on the beach, with one steep winding track leading to family settlements and farms inland. Horses are the only form of transport on the island. The islanders hold horse races in their spare time, and, to keep them as tough and wiry as their owners, stallions are encouraged to fight. Blood is often drawn, but the horses are separated before serious injuries occur.

Peninsular South Sulawesi has been settled for a very long time. Remnants of prehistoric culture there go back to at least the Middle Stone Age. These negative hand prints (right) were made about 5000 years ago by placing the hands against the rock and spitting a mixture of red ocher and water around them. They are part of a group of cave paintings found at Leang-Leang near Masor, 35 kilometres north of Ujung Pandang.

A child (above) plays in the water at Sinkang, South Sulawesi. The houses in her kampung sit on stilts over the water. Another Bugis village (left) nestles at the foot of a huge rock on the way up the peninsula toward Tana Toraja.

A young Bugis woman (right) lights up the morning with her smile.

A Tolaki man from Kendari, the provincial capital of Southeast Sulawesi.
Twin-sailed, twin-hulled sailing vessels, quite different in appearance from the Bugis prahu pinisi, are common in this area.

Volleyball, one of the most popular sports in Indonesia, is played here in a small Tolaki village. The "spiker"—the boy about to hit the ball—is wearing his father's Haji hat.

Pepper (below) is one of a dozen different crops grown on this fertile peninsula, but the area is best known for its large and tasty cashew nuts.

A woman grinds coffee beans (left) in a small Tolaki village north of Kendari. To and Toh are prefixes used throughout Sulawesi; they mean "person" or "man". Tolaki means "big man" in the local language, and probably refers to this group's prowess as headhunters in days gone by. Today the Tolaki are predominantly Muslim.

This modern young woman favours short hair and her father's shirts worn over baggy jeans, but carefully follows her mother's teachings on Tolaki dress and behaviour for formal occasions. The required jewellery includes dozens of heavy gold bangles.

159

A wedding guest, Kendari, Southeast Sulawesi. At Kendari weddings it is customary for the families of the bride and groom to engage speakers who extol the virtues of the individuals they represent. These two splendidly-dressed men spoke on behalf of the bride several weeks before the wedding at a ceremony to commemorate the symbolic payment of the bride price. The payment consisted of simple jewellery, lengths of cloth, a porcelain bowl and two young coconut trees. The bride and groom did not meet in public until the wedding itself.

The peoples of the islands off the southeast coast of Southeast Sulawesi, Buton, Muna, Tomea and the Tukangbesi Islands, all speak closely related languages and share a common culture. Their strongest affinities are with the Tolaki on the mainland. A silent family (above), not a smile among them, waits for the ship that will bring their son and brother back to Muna from the island of Buton. A somewhat friendlier figure (left) waits his turn during communal bath time on Tomea. Men and women share bathing facilities, everyone modestly covered in towels or sarongs.

The Sultan of Wolio ruled the island of Buton until the
Dutch took over direct rule in 1908. This men's dance,
held on the grounds of the Sultan's fort at Bau Bau on the
southwest coast, depicts the defeat of an invading force.
A closer view (far left) of a dancer's head-dress. Though
only spectators, the women all wear ceremonial dress.

A traditional women's dance (above) is performed on the
island of Tomea.

Low tide, Tomea. These boats
have been made in the same
manner for centuries. The use of
nails instead of wooden dowels has
only recently become common.

A smiling mother and child after
their afternoon bath.

Nusa Tenggara

Nusa Tenggara. The forgotten islands, a necklace archipelago stretching from Lombok all the way to Timor. Although taken all together these islands comprise less than four percent of Indonesia's land area, they contain such ethnic, cultural and linguistic variety that it is difficult to speak of them as a group. On the tiny island of Roti, for instance, there are nine distinct dialects spoken, and each of the island's eighteen states has a different culture. A few things can, however, be said of Nusa Tenggara in general. The majority of the people in this part of Indonesia are Christian rather than Muslim. The islands are all hot and dry, heavily influenced by the dessicating east monsoon which sucks moisture out of the land and air. Every year, between the planting of crops and their harvesting, many people endure what they call *lapar biasa*, the "usual hunger". When the west monsoon fails, as it does too often for anyone's comfort, the people endure a situation bordering on famine.

The people of Nusa Tenggara, especially those on the large islands of Sumbawa, Sumba, Flores and Timor, practice shifting-field slash-and-burn agriculture. As the fields become exhausted more land must be farmed to gain a sufficient crop for survival. On Sumba and Timor the situation has been aggravated by the raising of horses and cattle for export, which has resulted in the need to spend long, expensive, unproductive hours fencing the cropland to protect it from livestock. Erosion, a serious problem all through these islands, has been made worse by over-grazing. The major crops are corn and rice, grown by the dry-field method in most places because water is scarce. So much effort is needed to fence, work and protect the fields that there is little time to engage in other food-production activities, such as fishing. And because the cattle raised here are not, for the most part, consumed locally, they do not significantly improve the diet of the common people, which is often poor in protein and only barely sustaining.

On two small islands of the outer arc of Nusa Tenggara, however, the economic situation is considerably better. Savu and Roti, called by one ethnographic wit "the islands of non-eating people", depend heavily on the products of the lontar palm for their subsistance. Obvious uses for the leaves and wood of this tree include houses, furniture, musical instruments, mats, baskets and even cigarette papers. But the people of Savu and Roti take their exploitation of the lontar palm a giant step farther. They tap the sweet juice of the palm and drink it, either fresh or boiled into a syrup and diluted with water. The juice can be further reduced by boiling into palm sugar. The froth from the boiling juice is fed to the pigs, thus directly converting palm sap to protein. The consequences of their dependence on the lontar have been sweeping. First, and perhaps most important, there is no annual period of hunger on Roti and Savu. Any

A fisherman from Endeh, Flores, resting on one of the smaller islands of West Nusa Tenggara.

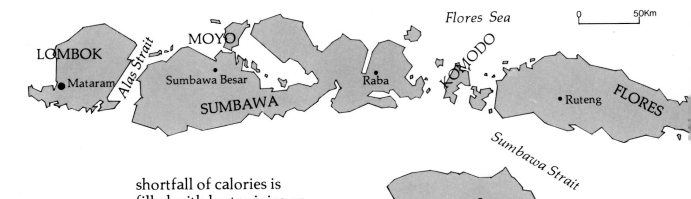

shortfall of calories is
filled with lontar juice or
syrup. Protein is supplied by
the syrup-fed pigs which most
families keep for their personal use.
The pigs, as well as the goats also kept
on the two islands, do not roam free, but are
penned or corralled, so valuable time is not wasted
fencing the fields. For optimal production of juice
the lontar palm must be selectively pruned. The leaves
are not discarded, but are used for fertiliser, enriching the
soil. Because the fields do not become infertile, shifting agriculture has
been replaced by semi-permanent garden plots, more productive and
less time-consuming to farm than the fields fertilised only by burning.

All these changes in work style, brought about by dependence
on the lontar palm, have had a further consequence on Roti and Savu
that has reverberated through the nearby islands. Palm-tapping,
although labour intensive for two to three months each year, does not
require much labour through the rest of the year. As much of the
garden work and weaving of lontar leaves is done by women, the men
have whole blocks of leisure time during the year which they can
devote to non-agricultural, non-subsistance activities. They also,
because the lontar palms never fail as a source of food, have the
resources to take economic risks. The men of Savu and Roti, there-
fore have become the entrepreneurs of the East Nusa Tenggara
islands, especially on Sumba and Timor.

Lontar is a drought-and fire-resistant tree that springs up on
fields already exhausted by slash-and-burn farming. It is thought that
the small islands of the outer arc, more exposed to forces of erosion
than are Sumba and Timor, became infertile sooner. The people
gradually learned to use the palms that colonised their exhausted
farmland. As erosion and soil-exhaustion take their toll on the large
islands, lontar palms are growing there, too, in some places nearly as
densely as they grow on Roti and Savu. But there is little opportunity
for the people of Timor and Sumba to gradually move towards
exploitation of the palm, because migrants from Savu and Roti have
filled that niche in the economy. The two sets of islands are already in
economic conflict, and the resolution is not yet clear.

Although life can be difficult in Nusa Tenggara, there is a
richness of culture here found in few places on earth. One of the area's
most striking cultural characteristics is the prevalence of traditional
hand-woven textiles using a technique called *ikat*. Unlike supplementary weft, a more widespread and probably newer technique in
which extra weft threads are woven in patterns, in *ikat* the threads
themselves are dyed in patterns before being tied on the loom to form

Larantuka • | SOLOR | ADONARA | LOMBLEN | • Kalabahi | ATAURO
Lewoleba | PANTAR | ALOR

Savu Sea

h

Ombai Strait | • Dili | • Manatuto | Lospalos
• Sare | R. Belulic | • Viqueque
• Same

TIMOR

• Cailaco
• Maliana

Timor Sea

• Kupang

Seba

AVU | ROTI

the warp. *Ikat* is a technique that probably entered Indonesia during the late Neolithic period. The process of dying the threads is long and complex. A textile made with natural dyes can take several years to complete. *Hinggi*, the rectangular two-panelled textile worn by men on Sumba for instance, usually takes two years.

Weaving is an important art in many areas in Indonesia, and hand-woven textiles have always played a vital role in Indonesian society, especially in the ceremonies connected with rites of passage—birth, puberty, marriage and death. Textiles are intimately connected with the forming of marriage ties and are part of a girl's dowry in most parts of the archipelago. They circulate as gifts during the negotiations between families and at the wedding itself. Most Timorese textiles, for instance, are used in gift exchanges between bride-givers and bride-takers. A wealthy bride's family would be expected to give more than a hundred pieces of weaving. In some parts of Timor textiles are hung before the doors leading to the bride's room; as the groom moves through the house he has to "buy" his way through the cloth barriers between him and his bride. Equally important is the use of textiles at funerals. On Timor warp *ikat* cloths are used to cover the coffin before burial; on Flores traditional shawls are buried with the dead. On Sumba the dead are often buried with large quantities of *hinggi*.

Cloths are important symbols of status and prestige in the Eastern Islands. The number and quality of textiles owned tends to indicate social rank. To some extent this can be explained purely in economic terms: The weaving of *ikat* textiles, exclusively the task of women, is a time-consuming occupation. The better the textile, the longer the time needed to make it. Although most women weave, only families with sufficient resources to allow much time at the loom can accumulate large stores of fine-quality textiles.

Designs are often indicative of status, and in former times only the rulers could wear cloths with particular designs. The lion and stag motifs on cloths from Sumba were worn only by the elite. *Hinggi* with a broad white centre band were reserved for the raja. In the Lio area of Flores, the size, colour and pattern of the complicated *ikat* shawls

169

worn on ceremonial occasions denoted the status of the wearer. As well as status, design and colour sometimes reflect the wearer's place in society. On Timor, among the Atoni, where many different techniques of weaving are practised, the designs and manner in which they are arranged on the cloth are distinctive to the ten princedoms that once divided the area. To the Timorese, local textiles are a clear indication of one's area of birth and traditional allegiance. On Savu, each person belongs to the father's clan and to one of two other groups determined by the mother. These are called the greater blossom and the lesser blossom. It was once possible to know merely by looking at the colour of a ceremonial textile which blossom affiliation a person had. Today ordinary and ceremonial patterns are mixed together and no longer reflect social division.

Culture in Nusa Tenggara is by no means restricted to weaving; traditional ceremonies and ways of life still flourish almost unchanged. Because this part of Indonesia is resource-poor and industrially still underdeveloped, the modern world has encroached here less than perhaps anywhere else in the archipelago, but progress, with all its blessings and problems, is slowly making itself felt throughout these eastern islands.

A group of musicians on the island of Savu wait for the dancing to begin. The people here are justifiably proud of their musical traditions; all instruments and costumes are locally made.

OVERLEAF: *Komodo village on Komodo, a tiny island between Sumbawa and Flores. Originally settled by convicts from Flores, this is the dry desolate home of Indonesia's famous Komodo dragon. Because the island's rainfall is too sparse for rice cultivation, the staple diet of the villagers is fish.*

Sailing boats enter the sheltered waters near the island of Komodo. Fishermen are not the only visitors, however. The island is becoming a popular stop for tour boats from Bali. A Komodo mother covers her face in laughter as her two daughters, one a lovely teenager and the other a toddler, stand by. Having recovered her poise but with her smile intact, the same woman (right) exemplifies the island's recent prosperity.

Komodo island is literally crawling with dragons, giant reptiles related to monitor lizards. A young dragon (left) still shows the colours it was born with; older dragons are dark green. In olden days, goats were used to appease the dragons and keep them away from the village, where they occasionally raided the local livestock. Today interested tourists can watch as they devour their prey. Altogether thirteen dragons, some nearly four metres long, turned up to feast on this single goat. A villager, by now accustomed to the sight of strangers, offers a carved dragon for sale. He tells the tale of a huge beast living in the hills whose likeness he has carved.

176

Flores is known for the high quality of its textiles, especially warp ikat, in which the pattern is dyed into the warp threads before they are woven. Although synthetic dyes and machine-spun imported cotton are making inroads here, locally-grown cotton, cleaned and spun by hand, is still in use. A woman uses a small hand-operated "gin" (right) to remove the seeds from raw cotton prior to spinning. The spun cotton will be bundled, tightly tied and then dyed before being wound onto the loom. The weaver uses a plain weave with unpatterned thread to complete the textile. As is the case with many Indonesian textiles, good Flores cloths are becoming rare.

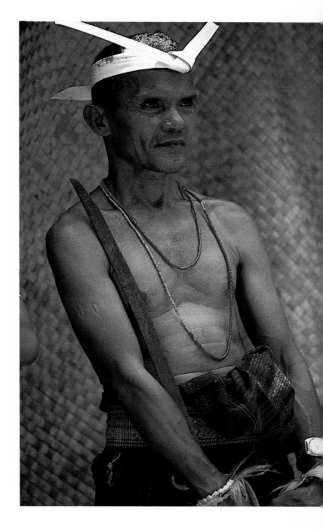

Lewo Leba, in the hills near Larantuka, East Flores, offers a spectacular welcome to guests of the village. First comes an aggressive war-like dance and an exchange of greetings. Then all guests file past a welcome line (left). Betel nut and lime are offered, but one may politely refuse by touching the carved container and continuing down the line. A distinguished-looking man wearing a large wristwatch waits for his entrance in a dance; and a girl takes part in a dance performed by women on ceremonial occasions.

Horses play an important part in the life and culture of Savu. These are being ridden in the Perhere Jara, a dance which enacts the use of horses to chase away grasshoppers during the rainy season. Horses are also ridden down to the beach to welcome guests arriving by boat.

Savu is not merely an island, it is an island kingdom. The Queen (left) is escorted to a place of honour in the shade.

A Savu girl (right), with a fighting cock under her arm, takes part in a local dance-drama. Cock fighting is also used to cast omens on Savu. One cock represents land, the other sea. If sea wins, the omen is bad; if land wins, the omen is good.

Perhaps because of its inaccessibility, the inhabitants of Savu still enjoy a rich ceremonial life. The Pedoa dance (above) is usually danced in moonlight between March and May. This is a harvest dance, and unhusked rice is in the baskets tied to the dancers' ankles. In the Dabba, or blessing ceremony for a child (far left), the parents place betel nut and flowers on the child's head and "hope that he will grow".

A young man (left) takes part in a dance-ceremony which tells the story of the end of war on Savu: fighting between men with swords gave way to cock-fighting with fowl owned by opposing villages. Cock-fights gave way in turn to a peaceful, enlightened time when only dances performed by girls with feathers serve as a remainder of Savu's fierce and warlike past.

A Savu-style "Joe Cool" lounges on a street in Seba, the island's main village.

Thatched huts in the village of Taraka, near Kupang, West Timor.

East Timor, Indonesia's 27th province, is an unknown area to most tourists and to many Indonesians as well. A woman (far left) from the village of Sare pounds corn in a hollow tree trunk to separate the kernels from the cob. The kernels will be placed in the small baskets at her feet and tossed in the air to remove the chaff. She is sitting in front of a palm-frond shed used to store seed corn. Men (bottom left) carry beef ribs to market at the town of Maliana.

Because there is no farmland on the tiny island of Atauro, the government is encouraging families to move to Timor. One hundred families totaling nearly seven hundred people have been resettled in the new village of Cailaco. Upon arrival each family receives one-half hectare of land on which to grow corn, and a one-room house. Another half-hectare will be added later, along with government assistance in growing rice. This family arrived in the resettlement village only three weeks before the photograph was taken. The young girl is the only member of her family to speak Bahasa Indonesia. Her parents, grandmother and little brother speak only the dialect of their former home.

Maluku

Maluku. The legendary Spice Islands, fought over for centuries by a Europe desperate for the cloves and nutmeg needed to preserve their meat. The islands that make up this province cover an immense amount of water, but, taken all together, make up only a tiny fraction of Indonesia's land mass. They stretch from Halmahera in the north, shaped like Sulawesi in miniature, to the eastern tip of Timor in Nusa Tenggara. Historically the most important islands in the province are Ambon, the tiny island of Ternate just west of central Halmahera, and the Banda Islands in Central Maluku south of the island of Seram. These three, along with Tidore, Ternate's rival power in North Maluku, bore the brunt of European contact—first Portuguese and Spanish, then Dutch—that started in the 15th Century and continued into the 20th. Before that time, Maluku was well known to Indian, Chinese and Arab traders who, like the Europeans, valued the spices grown there.

Maluku lies squarely within the "Ring of Fire"; volcanic eruptions and earthquakes are common. Its wildlife, studied by A.R. Wallace, an influential in forming his theory of evolution in the 19th Century, is more similar to that of New Guinea and Australia than of western Indonesia. The crops that made the area famous, cloves and nutmeg, along with cocoa, and coffee, are still major crops. Although rice is grown on some islands, notably Seram, the staple diet of most people is sago, reduced to flour and then boiled into a viscous paste. Fish is also an important item, and some of the world's richest fishing grounds surround these islands.

Very little is known about Maluku prior to the 15th Century. The Muslim empire of Ternate, which dominated the spice trade before the arrival of the Portuguese, reduced the incidence of headhunting and introduced political rather than tribal social organisation on some of the islands, especially the island of Ambon. There was, however, nothing approaching political unity. When the Portuguese conquered Goa and Malacca in the first decade of the 16th Century, Maluku was known as *Jazirat-al-Muluk*, the "land of many kings".

Ambon, which at that time grew neither cloves nor nutmeg, had long been an important way-station in the spice traffic between the Banda Islands and Ternate. With the establishment of a Javanese colony centuries earlier in the town of Hitu on the northern coast of Ambon, a pattern developed that was to be repeated all over Maluku: sailors and traders, usually from off-island, settled on the coasts, while the indigenous peoples moved inland. Their lives were unchanged by the passage of time as they followed their own traditions in the interior. They were called *Alifuro* by the newcomers, a contemptuous term meaning uncouth, uncultured and uncivilised. This attitude has changed little during the intervening years. Now,

A man from the forested regions of the island of Seram, Central Maluku.

187

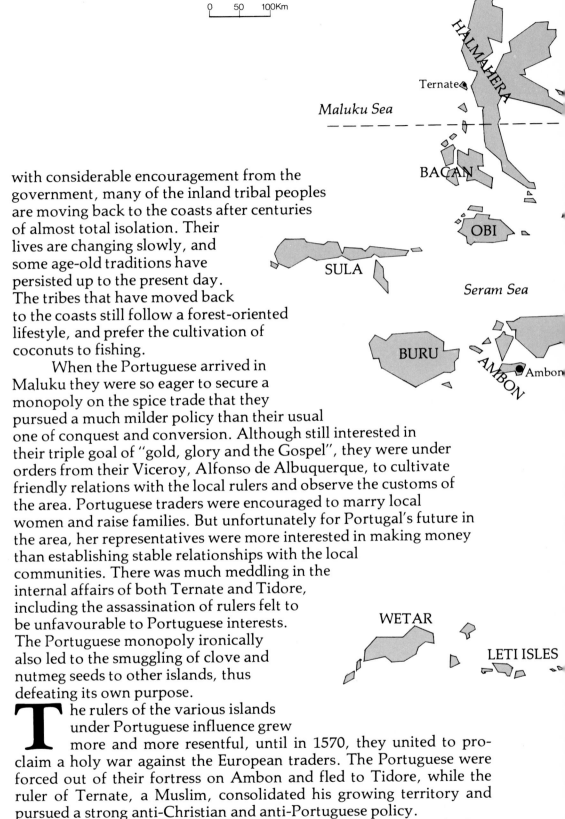

with considerable encouragement from the government, many of the inland tribal peoples are moving back to the coasts after centuries of almost total isolation. Their lives are changing slowly, and some age-old traditions have persisted up to the present day. The tribes that have moved back to the coasts still follow a forest-oriented lifestyle, and prefer the cultivation of coconuts to fishing.

When the Portuguese arrived in Maluku they were so eager to secure a monopoly on the spice trade that they pursued a much milder policy than their usual one of conquest and conversion. Although still interested in their triple goal of "gold, glory and the Gospel", they were under orders from their Viceroy, Alfonso de Albuquerque, to cultivate friendly relations with the local rulers and observe the customs of the area. Portuguese traders were encouraged to marry local women and raise families. But unfortunately for Portugal's future in the area, her representatives were more interested in making money than establishing stable relationships with the local communities. There was much meddling in the internal affairs of both Ternate and Tidore, including the assassination of rulers felt to be unfavourable to Portuguese interests. The Portuguese monopoly ironically also led to the smuggling of clove and nutmeg seeds to other islands, thus defeating its own purpose.

The rulers of the various islands under Portuguese influence grew more and more resentful, until in 1570, they united to proclaim a holy war against the European traders. The Portuguese were forced out of their fortress on Ambon and fled to Tidore, while the ruler of Ternate, a Muslim, consolidated his growing territory and pursued a strong anti-Christian and anti-Portuguese policy.

The Portuguese never recovered their power, and their missionary activities, which had flourished under the influence of the charismatic Jesuit St. Francis Xavier, declined. Other European nations began to arrive in the area. Sir Francis Drake stopped at Ternate in 1579 and the first Dutch fleet come to Ambon in 1599. In 1605 the Portuguese surrendered their interests to the Dutch, after making what provision they could for the protection of Catholic

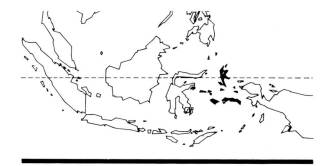

Equator

anahera Sea

RAM

WATUBELA ISLES

Neira

BANDA ISLES

Banda Sea

TOYANDU

KAI ISLES

ARU ISLES

TANIMBAR ISLES

or Sea

converts on the islands. The English returned, to the great aggravation of the Dutch, and set up a factory on the Island of Run in the tiny Banda islands. This group's largest island, Banda Neira, was to be the scene of one of the bloodiest chapters in the history of Dutch colonial rule in Indonesia.

When the Dutch first came to Banda Neira, the local population had for centuries been selling spices to regional Bugis, Chinese and Arab traders in return for batik, porcelains, rice, calico and medicine. The Dutch, unaware of local preferences, brought velvets, damasks and heavy woollens, as well as gunpowder, mirrors and other trinkets not particularly valuable or interesting to the people of Banda. They refused to indulge in the age-old practice of bargaining and, in return for their inappropriate and unwanted trade goods, demanded the island's entire crop of nutmeg, mace and cloves. Finally, to compound what must have appeared to the Banda rulers an already mind-boggling piece of idiocy, they insisted on putting their demands in writing to be signed by the Banda village chiefs. What followed was a classic case of culture clash, with neither side at all understanding what the other was about. For the people of Banda the results were tragic in the extreme.

The village chiefs first signed the Dutch agreements out of an embarrassed sense of courtesy in the face of ill-mannered insistance. They clearly had no intention of selling their entire crop at low and non-negotiable prices to be paid for in undesirable goods. They did not know that to the Dutch the documents had the weight of law behind them and could be enforced. Such a notion of law was inconceivable on Banda, where people lived in close-knit village communities presided over by *orang kaya*, "rich men", according to rules made by concensus and backed by centuries of tradition. The rich men politely and perhaps a little nervously signed the treaties, and then went on as they had always done, selling spices to their traditional buyers and adding to their clients the British on Run Island.

The Dutch threatened reprisals, and forced on the Bandanese a series of increasingly harsh and restrictive agreements, which the Banda nutmeg growers virtually ignored. In 1609 the Dutch East India Company sent a fleet and 750 soldiers to build a massive fort on Banda Neira which still stands today. The rich men and their families retreated to the hills, from whence they attempted to negotiate with the Dutch. They asked for hostages to guarantee Dutch good faith and arranged a meeting with the Admiral of the fleet. The Admiral agreed and, with most of his men, was killed in a Bandanese ambush. The consequences were catastrophic. In 1621 the Company Governor General in Batavia Jan Pieterszoon Coen sailed for Banda, determined to secure once and for all the monopoly on the Maluku spice trade. On his instructions, the rich men who had violated Dutch agreements along with most of the Bandanese population were murdered or transported as slaves. Nutmeg groves on all but the two main islands were destroyed in order to keep the supply down and prices up. Villages were razed and burned, and the few people who survived died of starvation or exposure in the hills. Of the Banda Islands original 15,000 inhabitants, a mere thousand remained.

In order to work the nutmeg trees on this now unpopulated archipelago, Coen divided the groves into concessions and offered free land grants to anyone who would, using imported slave-labour, tend the trees and process the nutmeg and mace, delivering the crop to the Company at fixed prices. Thus, after several stormy generations, Banda returned to a state of relative peace and affluence which lasted up to the mid-19th Century. By that time the nutmeg seeds which the British had shipped to plantations in Ceylon, Sumatra, Africa and Malaya reached maturity, and the Dutch monopoly was broken. Finally the advent of refrigeration, which provided a means of keeping meat edible without the heavy use of cloves and nutmeg, greatly reduced the world's demand for spices and ended forever the importance of Banda in the international arena. Ironically, although the Spice Islands are famous the world over, today they form a quiet backwater, neglected by the rest of the world, where the large and gracious mansions of the colonial Dutch crumble into ruin.

Women from a village near the south coast of Seram returning from their gardens. Common belief has it that these people, who call themselves Naulu, were the original inhabitants of the island. They were pushed inland by successive arrivals of outsiders.

OVERLEAF: *The sunsets over the eastern islands of Indonesia have a character all their own. This one is on the island of Tayandu, southeast Maluku.*

At lunchtime in a market on the island of Ambon, this woman does a brisk trade in snacks of rice and vegetables. The food is heated on the spot and wrapped in a banana leaf. Men about town idle on an Ambon street corner. The language may differ, but graffiti is the same the world over.

A fisherman mending his nets, Ambon island, and a view along Ambon's peaceful north-coast shoreline.

A group of men from a Naulu village in south central Seram. Others of their village were building a new village near the beach. Because their original home was deep inland, the villagers pursue a living in the forest rather than on the waves, cultivating coconut and roots of various types. These men were quite happy to have their pictures taken, but the older and generally more conservative people back at the village were reluctant and did not permit any women to be photographed.

Following a practice common throughout much of Indonesia, this shy little girl has her head shaved to keep it clean and to ensure that when hair does grow it will be strong and healthy.

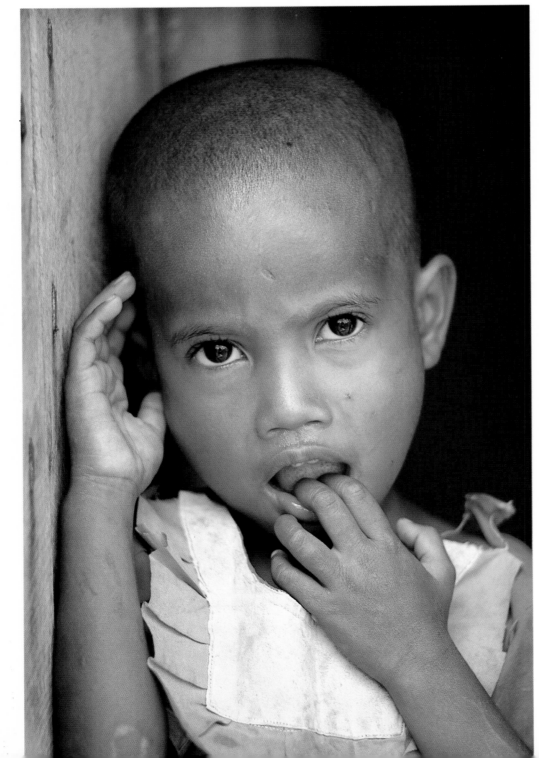

In a town on the south coast of Ambon (right), a man is on his way to market to pick up some vegetables, which he will carry on either end of the pole over his shoulder.

196

A Seram woman from a group who call themselves Naulu Nuelu. Their village is near the centre of the island, now more easily accessible by means of the trans-Seram highway which will aid development on the north coast.

An Ambonese becak driver, stylishly if unseasonably dressed in a bright plaid scarf, waits at the mini-bus station at Makariki on Seram. He has come because there is less competition here than on Ambon, where a great oversupply of becaks has led to the use of a rota system. In Kota Ambon becaks are colour-coded red, yellow, green or blue and only allowed to carry passengers on the days designated for each colour.

Cloves and nutmeg made the islands of Maluku famous and gave them the name Spice Islands. Nutmeg trees are dioecious—there are both male and female trees — and grow to a height of twelve to fifteen metres. The ripe fruit (far left) has been broken open to reveal the hypocotyl of scarlet mace wrapped around the shiny chestnut-coloured nutmeg seed.

The Dutch fort was built on the ruins of a 16th-Century Portuguese fort on the island of Banda Neira. When the Dutch took control of Banda in the early 17th Century, the Governor ordered the death of many of the influential people on the islands in order to gain control of the nutmeg trade. The Banda islands are still the world's major supplier of nutmeg.

The brown booby (below) a common sight in Maluku.

When the Dutch finally evicted the Portuguese from Banda, they had been there for nearly a century, and the local dances show a distinct Portuguese influence. The helmets, shields shaped like blunderbusses, even the costumes reflect the island's past. By contrast, this rather odd presentation of a tale about a mythical beast bears some resemblance to a Chinese dragon dance. The dancers are for the most part children dressed in sackcloth and wearing papier-maché masks, as does the beast. At night, village men dance around a large bronze drum decorated with leaf offerings.

203

On Tayandu, a tiny island in the Kai archipelago near Irian Jaya, there is a thriving pottery industry. Both the clay and vegetable colouring used in these pots are locally produced. The potter's wheel is unknown here. Pots are hand built, then dried and fired in small wooden ovens on the blisteringly hot beach. Sold cheaply to passing boats, they are a fine example of village craft.

Traders seeking spices in Southeast Maluku brought their religion with them. On Pulau Kasiui, Watubela Islands, the people are all Muslim. This old man wears a white hat, indicating that he has made the pilgrimage to Mecca and may use the title Haji.

On the verandah of the island's only mosque, a drum summons the faithful to prayer before the voice of the Muezzin calls from the minaret. In cities the Muezzin's call is often taped and broadcast by loudspeaker.

Irian Jaya

Irian Jaya. Not only a different place from the rest of Indonesia, but a different time as well. An enigmatic and difficult land that doesn't yield its secrets easily, virtually nothing about Irian Jaya is well understood. Like its other half, Papua New Guinea, Irian is geographically varied and scenically spectacular. Coastal swampland, broad highland river valleys, soaring mountains—even a glacier high in the central mountains. Except for the glacier, the island shares these features and an abundance of wildlife, much of it rare, with other parts of Indonesia.

What is strikingly different are the people. Culturally and ethnically, the Irian peoples are classified as Papuan, related to the Melanesoids of the South Pacific rather than the basically Malay people of island Southeast Asia. They are dark-skinned and heavily bearded, with facial features reminiscent of Australian Aborigines. This resemblance is not surprising as Australia and New Guinea were once a single land mass.

Because the terrain is so rugged, communities tend to live in isolation from one another, and there is little cross-communication. War is common in Irian Jaya, but it tends to be war between people in the same ethnic group rather than with outsiders. There is some outside trade, but mainly groups tend to keep to themselves. The rugged terrain also makes entry from outside extremely difficult, and not much is known about many of the Irian groups. Two that are relatively accessible, however, are the Dani of the Baliem Valley in the Central Highlands, and the Asmat of the southwest coast.

The Dani culture is in many ways incredibly primitive. The people have almost nothing in the way of technology—ten years ago all the tools were of polished wood, stone, bone or sharpened bamboo—and produce no art. They have a number system that goes from one to three; anything higher is "many". Their only domestic animal is the pig, which is valued at least as highly as the Dani woman. Pigs and shells are the two media of exchange in Dani society, and circulate freely at funerals, weddings and feasts. Examined closely, however, Dani technology and agriculture are more complex than they first appear. Although sweet potatoes are cultivated with only a digging stick, they are grown on raised plots surrounded by elaborate irrigation ditches. The ditches are also used as compost pits, and each new crop is started on well-fertilized soil. Tobacco and other garden crops are also grown on a small scale. Pigs are bred selectively; all but the best are castrated to increase their size.

The climate in the Baliem valley is temperate, but because the elevation is high it can get cold at night. Dani men's houses are divided into a lower level, with a fire pit, and an upstairs sleeping loft kept comfortably warm by the fire below. What smoke doesn't escape through the gaps in the bamboo and plank walls is useful in keeping

A grim-faced Asmat villager from southwest Irian Jaya.

207

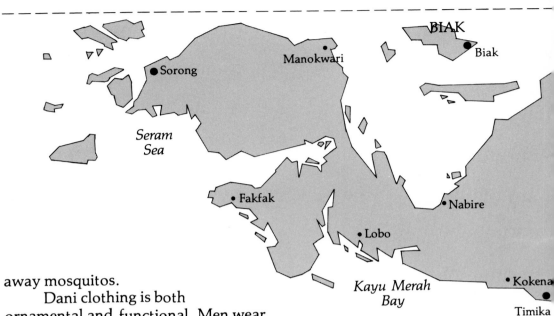

away mosquitos.

Dani clothing is both ornamental and functional. Men wear feather and shell ornaments and *Koteka*, penis sheaths made from gourds of various shapes and lengths, cultivated in gardens. Women wear rolled grass or reed skirts, and hang knotted string bags down their backs. These bags are used to carry everything from pigs and sweet potatoes to babies, and also protect the women's vulnerable backs from attack by ghosts which are likely to enter the body through the anus or the base of the throat. Necks are protected by shell ornaments or a kind of bib made of pigskin, worn fat side down. As protection against the cold, the Dani grease their bodies with a thick layer of pig fat.

Men and women in Dani society live very separate lives. The activities of men centre around the men's house and tend to be communal. Women spend their time in the sweet potato gardens and the cookhouse, working alone or with their young daughters. Although husbands and wives often have affectionate and harmonious relationships, interaction between the sexes is low key. One custom peculiar to the Dani is a five-year sexual abstinance after the birth of a child. No one seems very bothered by this practice, and it seems to be unfailingly observed. When asked why, the reply is usually that the "ghosts" demand it.

Although the Baliem Valley Dani have been exposed to increasing contact with outsiders, both Indonesian and foreign, their way of life has not changed a great deal. Police posts in the valley have helped diminish the incessant tribal wars, but war has turned out to be less central to Dani culture than was previously thought. The polished stone tools used for thousands of years in the Baliem valley are still being used and made, but steel axes and blades are increasingly popular. The Dani have little cash income to pay for such things. Self-sufficient in sweet potatoes and pigs, and trading salt and pigs to other tribes for forest products, they produce little extra that can be traded for currency. It is perhaps to their advantage that the Baliem valley has no easily exploitable natural resources bringing hoards of other Indonesians and foreigners to the area. The same cannot be said for the Asmat.

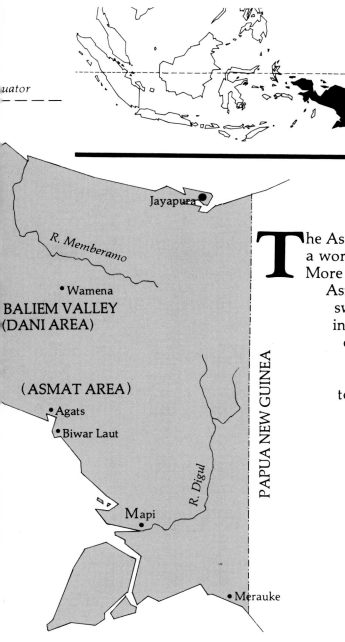

The Asmat live in lowland swamps, in a world that is half land, half water. More than six metres of rain falls on Asmat territory each year, and the swamps, stretching 70 kilometres inland, are inundated twice every day by the rising tide. When the waters receed, they expose a nighmarish tangle of tree roots to trap the unwary foot. Reptiles of every sort abound, and crocodiles are an ever-present menace. Travel is on foot or by canoe, paddled standing, with long, carved and decorated paddles. Since 1969, when what is now called Irian Jaya became a province of the Republic of Indonesia, many changes have taken place in Asmat culture. The most obvious is the banning of headhunting and inter-tribal warfare in the area, which has struck deep at the roots of Asmat tradition and way of life. Another subtler change, has been the development of permanent Asmat villages. Historically, temporary houses made of palm-leaf were the rule, used for about three months, then abandoned as food in an area was depleted. This practice still continues, but the Asmat are now required to visit their "villages" one or two days each week. Schools, hospitals and churches are all found in the villages, as are the men's ceremonial houses. The Asmat are pure hunter-gatherers, planting no crops, but roaming the tidal forests in search of sago, wild pig, lizards, insects, grubs, wild hen's eggs and edible plants. Sago is the staple, made into a flour and then roasted. Every four or five days a family fells a sago palm and spends the day processing the pith. Occasionally palms are felled and left in the forest for about six weeks to develop a good crop of capricorn beetle larvae, a great delicacy for the Asmat.

Like their Creator, who fashioned them from ironwood and brought them to life with the beat of a drum, the Asmat are master carvers. Their tribal art is considered some of the best in Oceania. Best known for two to three metre tall *Bisj* poles—tree trunks carved with crouching interlocked phallic figures—their ceremonial shields, paddles, sago bowls, and intricately carved prows for dugout war canoes are prized by collectors all over the world.

Under ordinary circumstances, Asmat men and women have little to do with one another. Women gather food, repair the houses, fish, cook and prepare sago. Men build the houses, hunt wild pig and, in former times, fought enemies and took heads. During the cycle of ceremonies that revolve around the carving of *bisj* poles, however, there is much stylised but cathartic contact between the sexes. During this time the men spend a lot of time in the forest choosing trees for carving, felling and decorating them. Each time they return to camp they are repulsed by the women, who attack them with stones, untipped arrows, and slung earth. These are mock battles, but a great deal of pent-up emotion is released.

Occasionally the Asmat practise a kind of ritual wife exchange for the purpose of tribal solidarity, creating pacts between men that last their whole lives. The men first agree to the exchange; then they pursuade their wives to agree. The women exchange houses for the night, cook the evening and morning meals for their new families, and then return to their original homes laden with gifts. In times of extreme stress—if, for instance, foreigners are seen in the village for the first time—or during *bisj* ceremonies an entire village may exchange wives, welding the village into single intimate unit.

Unlike the Dani, for whom tribal war was not irreplaceable, without war the Asmat have little motivation for art and cultural tradition. With luck and help from the authorities and missionaries in the area they may find another way to organise their lives that makes sense in their particular cultural context. In the meantime, their reaction to the outsiders who come into southwest Irian to exploit the timber, coal and copper is one of passivity. Although increasing sensitivity to their needs on the part of government officials in the area is mitigating to some extent their sense of cultural dislocation, the Asmat situation is still extremely difficult. Only the future will reveal if their cultural and artistic traditions, unique even in a country rich with such traditions, can adapt to the modern world.

Curious children gather on a jetty at Kayu Merah Bay to watch the arrival of visitors.

OVERLEAF: *The main street of the Asmat village of Biwar Laut, one of the villages visited by Michael Rockefeller shortly before his disappearance in 1961.*

These children live with their grandparents on a small island in the Triton Bay waterway just north of Kayu Merah Bay. Their parents work in Desa Lobo, a day's journey away by dugout canoe. Every fortnight the grandfather paddles to Desa Lobo to trade yams, fish and coconuts for supplies.

In the Triton Bay area the use of Western clothing is more common than in places less subject to outside contact. Some people, however, still prefer the older styles. This man was visiting the village for a day, perhaps to trade, perhaps only to look around. Despite pressure from missionaries and government personnel, he shows no inclination to change his ways.

Desa Lobo sits at the foot of Gunung Lobo, a sheer cliff face more than a thousand metres high. The whole Kayu Merah Bay area is alive with birds. Along with the crested tern shown here, birds spotted in a single afternoon include Blythe's hornbill, white-bellied sea eagle, sulphur-crested cockatoo, reef heron, black-naped tern, common sandpiper, whimbrel, Australian pelican, frigate bird and Brahminy kite.

Confronted by what is probably the largest vessel he has seen in his life, this lone boatman exhibits remarkable sang-froid. The contrast between their stone-age culture and the modern world is so shattering that many Irian natives, especially those of the older generation, respond to new wonders with a kind of not seeing, a refusal to integrate the unbelievable sights around them.

The Dani people inhabit the Baliem Valley in Irian Jaya's central highlands. In accordance with Dani mourning rituals, this old woman is missing several fingers. When a man dies, his close female relatives have one or more fingers amputated at the knuckle as a sign of grief. A Dani mother (right) with her child.

The dances of the Dani are quite elaborate. Villagers (above) enact the "Siege of the Chief's Pole"

A grieving widow (left) shortly after having one of her fingers amputated. The operation is performed with a sharp stone chopper, and the stump is dressed with a mixture of clay and ashes and a wrapping of husks and banana leaves. The widow, like all the female relatives of the deceased, has smeared her body with mud. When the mud dries it turns bluish white, giving her a ghostly pallor. She is accompanied by the chief's wife, who is also missing several fingers. Although ritual mutilation is now forbidden, the practice continues in remote areas.

The village chief wears only a hat, necklace and three-foot-long kote-ka. Made of hollow gourds and supported at the waist with twine, penis sheaths are standard dress for men in the Baliem Valley.

An Asmat woman (right) from the village of Biwar Laut. Classic hunter-gatherers, the Asmat live in the mangrove swamps of the south-west coast. They are taller and more angular than the highland Dani.

218

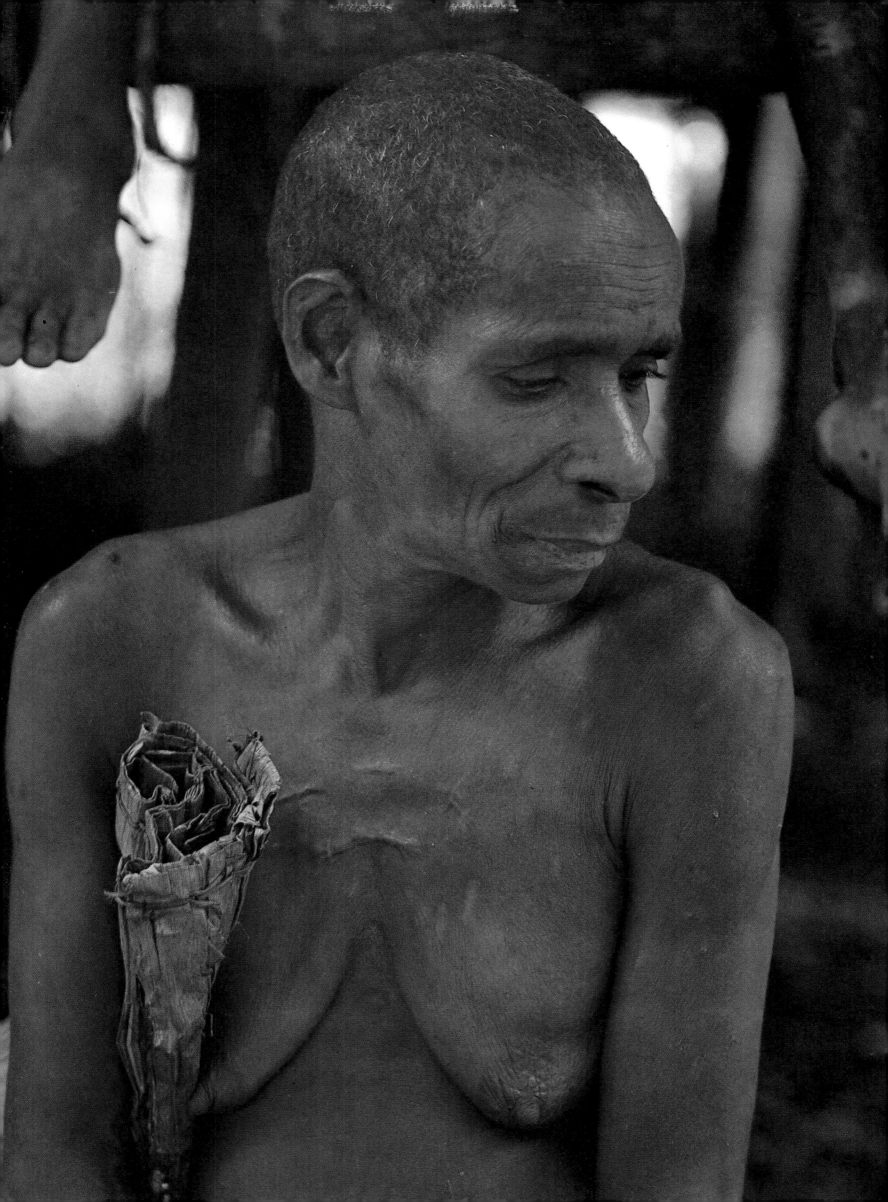

The traditional Asmat greeting at the mouth of the river for guests arriving by sea. All the men of Biwar Laut take part, and, should the visitors be unfriendly, their spears and perhaps the sharp ends of their paddles can be put to lethal use. The carved prow of the boat (below) typifies the care that the Asmat take in the things they make.

An Asmat adat *chief studies his unexpected visitors with dark piercing eyes. Another man turns up in full ceremonial regalia, including a shell nose ornament. Bone and bamboo nose ornaments are popular, as are headbands made from* kus-kus *fur and trimmed with cowrie shells, though these are generally worn only by men. Cowrie shells had the same history of use as currency here as in many other areas, notably East Africa and Polynesia. Now, however, they are only used as ornaments and for payment of the bride price.*

Head-on exposure to modern technology: listening to music on a borrowed tape player. This smiling mother wears a kus-kus *headband, which she would not do for a serious occasion.*

223

A Bisj pole, elaborately carved and dressed.
The Bisj ceremony is part of a cycle of rituals
performed on behalf of a dead man. Because its use
promoted tribal warfare, the ceremony was once
banned by the government. It has recently been
revived in a more peaceful context, as a purely
commemorative ritual.

An artist displays his shield. Used both ceremonially
and for war, these weapons are highly prized. Today,
however, many beautiful old pieces have left family
lineages to grace the shelves of collectors. In areas
where visitors are common, the standard of
workmanship is dropping in a bid to increase
production.

A village elder (right) sits on the welcome porch of the
men's house.

Three men wave a cheerful farewell from their dugout canoe. The pride and optimism of these people will stand them in good stead as they go through the changes ahead.

PHOTOGRAPHER'S NOTES

What started as an after-dinner conversation in 1980 has finally, after three years, eight thousand photos, two bouts of cholera, and who knows how many miles, become a finished product. It wasn't easy, but neither has it been dull. Indonesia is a fascinating, if often frustrating country to visit. Few people realise how vast it is until, as I did, they try to cross it from one end to the other.

Travelling in planes of all sizes, boats ditto, jeeps, mini-buses, on horseback and on foot, carrying my never-failing Hasselblads and Nikons, I gradually came to understand this vast country where I had spent so much time as a child.

For those readers who are camera buffs, I have included a list of equipment used in taking the photographs for this book:

Hasselblads, both the 500 C/M and the SWC/M, with lenses from the 38mm Biogon to the 250mm Sonnar. I also used the Nikon F3, F2AS and FE, all with motor drives to minimise missed shots and save time, with Nikkor lenses from the 20mm f3.5 to the 500mm f8 mirror. My favourite combination for people is the Nikon F3 with the 105mm f4 Micro-Nikkor lens.

PRODUCTION NOTES

The efforts of many people combined to produce this book, and much thought and care has been invested in it. For those who are interested a list of technical details follows:

The typeface used is Paladium T, set by Computype on a Compugraphic ACM 9000 Keyboard. Colour separations were by Colourscan made with a Hell Chromagraph DC 350 ER Laser Scanner. The book was printed by Tien Wah Press in fine screen (175 line per inch) lithographic process on a Heidelberg Speedmaster Press.

ACKNOWLEDGEMENTS

In a book of this nature it is never possible to acknowledge everyone who helped bring it to fruition.

Special gratitude, however is due to Ibu Dra. Cri Murthi Adi, Director of Marketing at the Directorate General of Tourism; Garuda Indonesian Airways; Lindblad Travel; and Mrs. Nora Suryanti, retired from the Ministry of Information. We would also like to thank P. Ngr. Ardika; Dr. Jacques Delmon; The Ganesha Volunteers; Linda Go; Mrs Lucy Lawalata; Karen Longeteig; Drs. Wahyono Martowikrido; Natour Hotels Indonesia; Nyoman S. Pendit; Ronald Shaw; Soedarmadji J.H. Damais; Dea Sudarman; Dr. Parsudi Suparlan; Sylvia The; and Drs. I.G.M. Wismaya.

The photographer would like to thank his parents for their faith and encouragement in his work.

Indonesians : Portraits from an Archipelago has been published under the auspices of the Indonesian foundation *Yayasan Bhakti Putra.* Established by the Mahendra family, this foundation will provide scholarships to promising Indonesians, at the high school or university level, for study within Indonesia or abroad. The photography in this book was funded by the foundation and forms the core of its photo-archives. The photographs are accessible to the public.

BIBLIOGRAPHY

The following books were used in the preparation of this book and may prove interesting to the general reader.

Abdurachman, Paramita R. "Moluccan Responses to the First Intrusions of the West". In *Dynamics of Indonesian History* edited by Haryati Soebadio and Carine A. du Marchie Servaas. Amsterdam: North-Holland Publishing Company, 1978.

Barnes, R.H. *Kedang: A Study of the Collective Thought of an Eastern Indonesian People.* Oxford: Clarendon Press, Oxford, 1974. Monographs on Social Anthropology.

Bartlett, Joe C.; Cale, Roggie; and George A. Fowler, Jr. *Java: A Garden Continuum.* Singapore, Amerasian, 1974.

Baum, Vicki. *A Tale From Bali.* 1937 Reprint. Kuala Lumpur: Oxford University Press, 1973.

Black, Star, and Stuart-Fox, David. *Bali.* Hong Kong: Apa Productions, 1980.

Caldwell, Malcolm, and Utrecht, Ernst. *Indonesia: An Alternative History.* Sydney: Alternative Publishing Cooperative, 1979.

Covarrubias, Miguel. *Bali.* 1937. Reprint. Kuala Lumpur: Oxford University Press, Oxford in Asia Paperbacks, 1972, 1981.

Dalton, Bill. *Indonesia Handbook.* Franklin Village, Mich.: Moon Publication, 1977.

dePanthou, Patrick, and Muller, Kal. *Bali.* Papeete: The Two Continents Publishing Group, 1978.

Duly, Colin. *The Houses of Mankind.* London: Thames and Hudson, 1979.

Fischer, Joseph. *Threads of Tradition: Textiles of Indonesia and Sarawak.* Berkeley: University of California & Fidelity Savings and Loan Association, 1979.

Fox, James J. *Harvest of the Palm: Ecological Changes in Eastern Indonesia.* Cambridge: Harvard University Press, 1977.

Geertz, Clifford. *The Religion of Java.* Chicago: The University of Chicago Press, 1960.

Gittenger, Matiebelle. *Splendid Symbols: Textiles and Tradition in Indonesia.* Washington, D.C.: The Textile Museum, 1979.

Hanna, Willard A. *Indonesian Banda: Colonialism and its Aftermath in the Nutmeg Islands.* Philadelphia: Institute for the Study of Human Issues, 1978.

Heider, Karl G. *Grand Valley Dani: Peaceful Warriors.* Case Studies in Cultural Anthropology, edited by George and Louise Spindler. New York: Holt, Reinhart & Winston, 1979.

Horne, Lee. "Rural Habitats and Habitations: A Survey of Dwellings in the Rural Islamic World". In *The Changing Rural Habitat*, Vol. II. (Proceedings of a seminar held by the Aga Khan Award for Architecture.) Singapore: Concept Media, 1982.

Horridge, Adrian. *The Prahu: Traditional Sailing Boat of Indonesia.* Kuala Lumpur: Oxford University Press, 1981.

Hutton, Peter. *Java.* Third Edition. Hong Kong: Apa Productions, 1978.

Koentjaraningrat, Ed. *Villages in Indonesia*, Ithaca: Cornell University Press, 1967.

Lebar, Frank, M, ed. *Ethnic Groups of Insular Southeast Asia. Vol. 1: Indonesia, Andaman Islands and Madagascar.* New Haven: Human Relations Area Files Press, 1972.

Lee Khoon Choy. *Indonesia: Between Myth and Reality.* Singapore: Federal Publications, 1977.

Loeb, Edwin M. *Sumatra: Its History and People.* 1935 Reprint. Kuala Lumpur: Oxford University Press, Oxford in Asia Paperbacks, 1972, 1982.

McPhee, Colin. *A House in Bali.* 1944 Reprint. Kuala Lumpur: Oxford University Press, 1979.

Pelzer, Dorothy W. *Trek Across Indonesia.* Singapore: Graham Brash, 1982.

Powell, Hickman. *The Last Paradise.* 1930 Reprint. Kuala Lumpur: Oxford University Press, Oxford in Asia Paperbacks, 1982.

Smithies, Michael. *A Javanese Boyhood: An Ethnographic Biography.* Singapore: Federal Publication, Federal Asian Library 1982.

Van Ness, Edward C. and Shita Prawirohardjo. *Javanese Wayang Kulit: An Introduction.* Kuala Lumpur: Oxford University Press, Oxford in Asia Paperbacks, 1980.

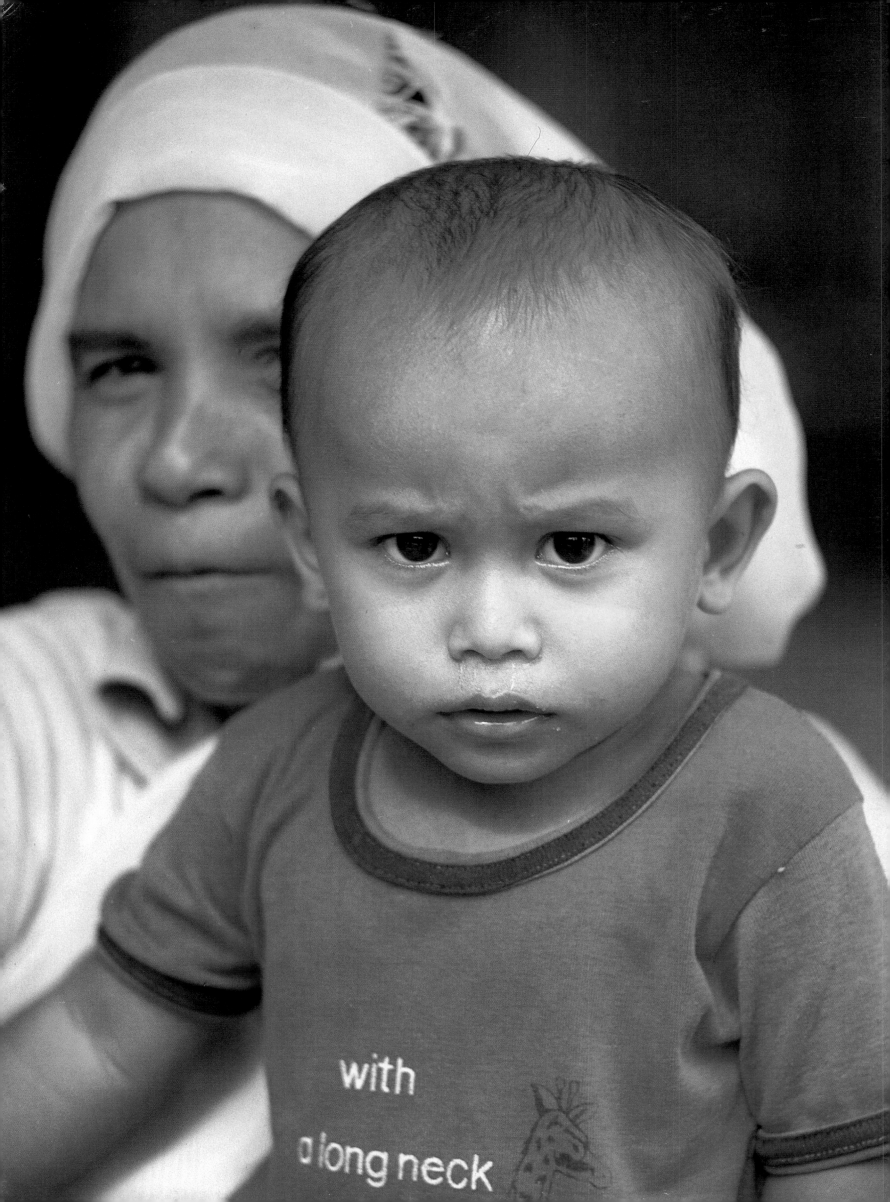

with
a long neck